Swerve

WHEN LIFE THROWS CURVES BUT GOD SAYS *Live*

KELLY CAPRIOTTI BURTON

PUBLISHED IN PARTNERSHIP.
Surfside Beach | Murrells Inlet
South Carolina

Kell {of a} Story

Greenfeet Publications
SENDING GOOD WORDS OUT TO THE WORLD

Copyright © 2022 by Kelly Capriotti Burton
All rights reserved. No part of this book may be reproduced in any manner whatsoever without written permission except in the case of brief quotations embodied in critical articles and reviews.

First Printing, 2022

"We Wait for You (Sehkinah Glory)"
Caleb Culver / Cory Hunter Asbury / Randy Matthew Jackson
Reckless Love lyrics © Bethel Music Publishing, Watershed Worship Publishing, Cory Asbury Publishing

Some scripture quotations from The Authorized (King James) Version. Rights in the Authorized Version in the United Kingdom are vested in the Crown. Reproduced by permission of the Crown's patentee, Cambridge University Press.

Scripture quotations marked MSG are taken from THE MESSAGE, copyright © 1993, 2002, 2018 by Eugene H. Peterson. Used by permission of NavPress, represented by Tyndale House Publishers. All rights reserved.

Scripture quotations marked (NLT) are taken from the Holy Bible, New Living Translation, copyright ©1996, 2004, 2015 by Tyndale House Foundation. Used by permission of Tyndale House Publishers, Carol Stream, Illinois 60188. All rights reserved.

Published by Kelly Capriotti Burton
Cover design by Kelly Capriotti Burton
ISBN: 978-1-7361174-2-2
ISBN EBook: 978-1-7361174-3-9

kellofastory.com | Surfside Beach, South Carolina
Greenfeet Publications | Murrells Inlet, South Carolina

Contents

Dedication	ix
Foreword	xiii
REDEMPTION The Disclaimer	1
AUTHENTICITY Connecting in a world that constantly tweaks us	5
VALIDATION An approval addict shows up for herself	10
MOM-PRENEUR LIFE Dealing with wrinkles	13
CHOSEN FAMILY Disinherited	17
FITNESS On renewal and transformation	21

GIFTS OF MARRIAGE   25
Steady on

NEW DREAMS   28
This is who you are

MISCARRIAGE PART 1   31
Laughing again

SUBMISSION   34
A food rebel surrenders

FITTING IN   39
A lesson from my daughter

INSECURITY   43
Just for a second

MIRACLES   47
The end of infertility

HELPLESSNESS   51
Foster families and failed fixes

FRIENDSHIPS   55
Leaning into the seasons and reasons

MISCARRIAGE PART 2   59
Faith for life

BLENDING FAMILIES   66
Happily-Ever-Afters for Complicated Relationships

REALISTIC ROMANCE Both sides of Johnny Castle	71
(RECKLESS) LOVE The Ultimate Romantic Hero	76
MISCARRIAGE PART 3 God Said LIVE	80
THE YEAR 2020 God Said *Swerve*	88
Resources	94
Acknowledgments	95
About the Author	96

Dedication

For *Pastors Tom and Terrie Wallace,*
who led me to my personal revelation of God's New Covenant
and the fullness of grace that Jesus offers. Through all of the
curves in the journey, and as one of life's greatest bonuses,
they also became my family.

In Memory of
Pastor Mike McGirt

You saw it. You declared it.
I will continue to believe it.
Just giving them Jesus... with love always, KB

Author's Note

Like life, this book is not linear or perfectly ordered. All events are taken from my real life, but not in their chronological sequence.

Some names and details have been changed to protect the privacy of others.

Foreword

Let me tell you about when I first met Kelly.

We both attended a moms group full of local moms of very young kids. We were all finding our way in motherhood and adult married life.

I remember our gravitation towards each other in friendship, specifically the day she felt it was time (and necessary) to share with me how she and Rod "began their lives together."

It almost felt like a confessional.

I honestly think she was pretty much expecting me to run and hide my chaste Christian values and save them for a friend that was a bit more "clean."

Rabbit Trail: Even typing these words makes me cringe as I consider how many times I've been dropped or excluded from friendship based on my mistakes (including that time when a coworker, who highly esteemed my-now-husband and his sincere love for Jesus, found out he and I were dating... she literally said out loud - in my presence - how she didn't understand why he would choose "a woman like me").

Let's just say the joke's on her, because 20 years later he and I are still very much in love, and I get to enjoy his incredible love for Jesus as well as his chiseled 8-pack stomach every single day (and night).

I digress... back to Kelly.

I remember Kelly's vulnerability in that moment of sharing, and how my heart actually drew nearer to her, not farther away.

Not in a way that excused her confessed sin, but in a way that forgave it.

I admired her bravery, but understood her shame.

And I knew Jesus did too - all I wanted to do was be like him at that moment. I just wanted to be his love towards her. I wanted to be what she needed me to be - an unconditional friend.

Little did I realize, however, that my desire to love her would eventually evolve into a friendship that has loved me so. Not only me, but my children as well.

Oh what our lives would have been without if I'd made a different decision.

I'm here to tell you that this book is just another extension of Kelly's God-kinda-love for us all, and a reminder of how deperately each and every one needs his amazing grace.

If there ever was a book highlighting the ginormous need for God's grace towards us, this is the one.

If there ever was a book displaying the need for us to generously extend that very same grace towards the other humans in our lives, this is it.

Kelly's words are a sweet, gentle invitation to:

Lay down what you think you know - about anyone...

Relinquish your limited knowledge about someone else's life or lived experience...

Give up needing to understand all there is to understand about someone's circumstances...

As a prerequisite for freely giving your love.

Instead, allow her words to pave a clear, direct path to catching a possible glimpse into why God so loved the entire world that he gave his only Son.

If we can learn a smidge of what Kelly has learned about the grace she needs to give, as well as receive, collectively we could literally change this broken world.

Literally change. the. world.

Let's do it together, OK?

~ Deanna

DEANNA MASON
Creator of Refreshed Moms
Founder of Needle Movers for Social Equity

1.
Redemption
the disclaimer

"WE HAVE BEEN SANCTIFIED THROUGH THE SACRIFICE OF THE BODY OF JESUS CHRIST ONCE FOR ALL."
HEBREWS 10:10 KJV

I don't even remember not being a Christian. In churchy-terms, I was Born Again at age seven. I always loved everything about attending church At age 17, I was singing in the choir, teaching the three-and-four-year-olds in Sunday School, and doing just about whatever else meant I could be there, in the building, in the mix of things.

As a young adult, I fully embraced all the extra, and even the bizarre, pieces of charismatic Church culture. If the altar was open for prayer, I was there begging God for something. If prayer requests were being taken, I had a few or at least an unspoken one. I prayed earnestly for the gift of speaking in tongues, not yet aware that the power of Holy Spirit is already inside all believers (this is not a theology book, so I will offer some references as to my beliefs in the appendix). I gave my enthusiasm and money to every special speaker that graced our stage. I broke a young man's heart and confused and hurt both of our families because of a misinterpretation of 2 Corinthians 6:14. I also trusted every pastor or person of authority, because

Swerve

I did not yet trust the voice of God inside of me. Because of this, I entered into adulthood perplexed, depressed, misguided, and continuing to look for love in all the wrong places.

I do not write this introduction to cast blame on any one spiritual authority or teacher. God knows and so many of us can attest that we were molded into a so-called Christian religion that was based on many things Christ did not actually bring to us, models of behavior, precepts, emotional torment, and selective loopholes that have nothing to with the New Covenant about which the Apostle Paul taught the Church.

That said, I lived my early 20s in a pit of my own making because I believed what I was taught. I wanted Jesus with my whole heart, but my heart was human. I did not know how to reconcile the zeal and love inside of me with a world that will readily turn it into something despicable or at least, unrecognizable. So while I worshiped God outwardly, secretly, I was searching for some romantic hero to fill the emptiness I still felt. I lived a truly double life, pursuing two different methods of fulfillment, and keeping all my romantic pursuits hidden from my church friends (well, except for the ones that were right in the pit with me).

As years passed, rock bottom met me more than once. As I matured, I found a new understanding of Jesus and His grace, a new church circle (much trial and error there), and finally, through more travail than all those other dating pursuits put together, the one who would be my life's romantic hero. Even that, a marriage to *the one my soul loves*, was fraught with a sinful and complicated beginning that had serious and lasting effects on other relationships in our lives: my husband was still married when our relationship began, and many people, unsurprisingly, found this impossible to forgive.

For several years, the beginning of our love story was indeed a disclaimer that I shared when new friendships with fellow Christians verged on the intimate. It felt like I *must* tell them, because surely they needed to know about my past in order to make an informed decision about whether to be my friend.

Sounds just like grace, doesn't it?

It was not until we moved our family away from the scene of our crimes, found another really new church circle, and received a true revelation of the fullness of grace that I stopped disclaiming. We are new creatures in Christ, right? And all means "all," right?

As I began putting this collection together, I asked a writer friend of mine to review several chapters. This person, not necessarily a person of faith but one of intellect and sensitivity, posed this question to me: *Will this [casual mention of your adulterous past] be off-putting to believers?*

At that point, I had so long and so completely put my past in the past – right where God leaves it – that I had to pause and really consider the question. Happily, this supposed non-believer gave me an answer, as well:

Now I'm thinking in this larger work, it belongs and sits just fine. Maybe better than fine. If someone wants to cast a stone, he or she is not getting the point. For someone who thinks maybe she deserves a stone or two, this book argues that they don't. So the formula works. I am presenting myself as an imperfect person (as we all are) whose faith offers a positive way to navigate life. And I'm inviting the reader - you, Friend - into the affirmations.

I suppose I cannot really say it any better. If disclaimers needed to be a thing among Christian friends, would we not all have a few? Does the Word not say that the accuser will be defeated by the blood of the Lamb and the word of our testimonies? (Revelation 12:11). I do not wear the redemption of my past sins like a badge of honor, but I do wear white garments because that is what Jesus gave me in exchange for them. And I will share how God both humbled my husband and me *and* gave us a happy, blessed union, because I know there are many people out there who have never forgiven themselves and they need this affirmation just as I did:

You cannot stray so far that you cannot be close to the Lord again.

Nothing you do will make Him stop loving you.

Though there may be unavoidable earthly consequences to our bad decisions, there is no capacity to God's forgiveness or even His blessings.

No sin, no shame, no swerve... nothing can separate us from His love.

Swerve: You do not have to continually pay penance, apologize for, or present your past sins to your new friends. You do not have to be ashamed. You don't even have to remember them.

Consider: Do loving parents want their children to constantly tell others of their past bad behavior? Of course not. God does not expect this from you.

Live: When it comes to sharing the power of our testimonies, we can be led by Holy Spirit to the right time, place, audience, and purpose, boldly proclaiming the work of God in our lives!

2. Authenticity

connecting in a world that constantly tweaks us

"WHEN SHE SPEAKS SHE HAS SOMETHING WORTHWHILE TO SAY, AND SHE ALWAYS SAYS IT KINDLY." PROVERBS 31:26 MSG

So many articles float around these days that begin with the phrase, "Ten Things Not to Say To A..."

The phrase concludes with terms such as: New Mom, Working Mom, Mom of Multiples, Mom of Child with Special Needs, Stay-At-Home Mom, Homeschooling Mom, Mom of Many Children, Mom of Only Child, Single Mom, Mom Wearing Leggings as Pants, Mom Singing Milli Vanilli in The Grocery Line...

You get what I'm saying?

I know many of these categories (and especially ones I have not listed), are sensitive areas. Fact is, unless we have walked in certain shoes, we have no idea what another mom is going through. Does that make it wrong to reach out in an attempt to connect?

I mean, I, too, could nit-pick. (On that note, I could write a list of Things Not to Say To A Mom Whose Toddlers Have

Swerve

Been Infested With Lice and She is Freaking Out About It, but that's another story). I could say, "You know, since you don't know anything about blended families, maybe you don't have the wisdom to make an observation about our custody arrangements" or "Why yes, as a work-at-home mom, I do sometimes need a babysitter because whether I take a call in an office building or my dining room, the person on the other end will hear when my two toddlers are shouting the lyrics to 'Elmo's World.'" (This was a much bigger deal before 2020 hit and everyone was working at home...)

And quite honestly, any number of people who choose to comment on second marriages, female pastors, and/or breastfeeding on demand, have gotten daggers from these eyes of mine.

But, I still have a concern: How many of these lists needs to be written, read, applauded, and shared, before we just... stop... saying... anything?

In a quest to be sensitive, I will only draw from my own experience. My journey through infertility was relatively short compared to others, and it inevitably had my fairy tale outcome. But in the meantime... there were two-and-a-half years of longing, negative tests, humiliating procedures, bad news from doctors, of at least 20 women I knew getting pregnant, and lots and lots and LOTS of unsolicited, well-meaning pep talks.

A random internet search brought me to a list of 10 things not to say to "your infertile friend." At casual glance, at least seven of those things were said to me multiple times, some even by my parents or my husband, who I know would not have intentionally hurt me, ever. Meanwhile, at the time I was walking through infertility, I was finishing my bachelor's degree and student teaching, so I constantly heard, "It will happen when you are done with school," as if that had anything to do with my uterine adhesions, hormonal imbalances, and non-functioning right fallopian tube. And because I was an involved stepmom, I also heard "At least you have J & P," as if their lives were my consolation prize.

I had people give me baby blankets and scripture verses. I received adoption agency referrals. I had several friends tell me with fear and trembling that they were pregnant with their second or third babies (those were the worst. It sucks when your friends think you won't be happy for them!) If I were going to make a top ten list, I suppose those things would be on it. But honestly, who needs it?

Would I rather my friends and family ignore my disappointment and pain? NO.

Would I rather those who cared about me not try to console me? NO.

Did some of those difficult comments eventually help me grow stronger, consider other points of view, or even just get over myself for a few minutes? Did some of them even turn out to be, gasp, true? ABSOLUTELY!

(I actually found out I was pregnant less than four months after finishing school, which was simultaneously humorous and maddening.)

I know that sometimes, well-meaning conversationalists end up saying all the wrong things. I am raising my hand here to that one. I was born to connect with everyone I meet, and so there are countless times I have said something and immediately wished that toothpaste could, in fact, be put back in the tube. I also subscribe to that Steel Magnolia theory that no one cries alone in my presence, so it is my tendency to want to comfort another person, whether she is dealing with a scary diagnosis for her child or a big career-and-childcare decision.

So, I encounter a woman walking through Walmart, on a Myrtle Beach Saturday, with five kids holding on to the cart and two in it, and she isn't screaming or shoving unpaid-for Goldfish in their mouths or possibly holding a Wiffle bat in a threatening position, and I say, "I don't know how you do it!" I am, of course, trying to say, "You rock, mama!" I certainly don't mean to be saying The Wrong Thing.

Because really, what is the right thing? It is to be silent?

If it is, then forget this whole thing, because if the new cultural paradigm is to avoid eye contact and any hope of encouraging others, then I'm challenging all of us to be big weirdos. We were created to connect, and as we grow older, we are called to pass on our accrued wisdom to help younger moms, and on occasion, to swallow our words and just be there.

I know that there are moms in situations when truly awful comments have been made to or around them by strangers. There are always rude, small-minded comments to go around, but chances are, the people who say them are not going to be reading parenting articles on their best day. I suppose my hope is that when another mom, especially in a friendly tone, comments on our children or our circumstances with any modicum of sympathy or kindness, we *gently* correct a misconception, or if too tired to do so, just toss our hair and move on.

(I mean, if I had a dollar for every person who called my youngest daughter a tomboy, or my long-haired son a Princess, I'd be buying both our dinners... on a Mediterranean cruise)!

The conclusion here: Let's stop with the lists, with tweaking everyone all the time. Let's carry on the conversation.

Presumptions and assumptions can be insensitive and rude, but someone not knowing us is not a crime, and someone trying to know us should be seen as a gift. Because, at least I believe with all my heart, as moms, we are in this together, and I would rather be surrounded by caring voices than cold silence any day.

Swerve: If you aren't sure you have the right words, start by simply being a loving presence for someone else.

Consider: Is there someone you're afraid to reach out to because you aren't sure what to say?

Live: Tell that person a simple "I'm thinking of you/praying for you/here for you." Then release them and see what happens next.

VAValidationN
3.

an approval addict shows up for herself

> "And I am certain that God, who began the good work within you, will continue his work until it is finally finished on the day when Christ Jesus returns."
> Philippians 1:6 NLT

For my first Mother's Day as a stepmom, my thoughtful husband bought me a Joyce Meyers book entitled *Approval Addiction*.

Gaining approval of others has been a lifelong struggle for me. It has been attributed by a therapist, my pastor, more than a handful of covenant friends, and obviously, my husband, that it is a result of some things like birth order, "second-born syndrome," if you will. I have many thoughts about the reasons why, and no doubts that the condition exists for me.

It was another book, read 15 years later, that helped me to truly make strides past my approval needs and deal with others' responses to me in a healthier way.

The Emotionally Healthy Woman by Geri Scazzero launched huge internal changes and several life choices for me; it is part of the reason you have this book to read right now!

Learning to quit harmful behaviors and thought patterns

changed the voices in my head. I quit doing certain things that produced toxic results for me, such as soliciting approval from people who knew they could manipulate me or apologizing for making my own self or family a priority. I quit on relationships that I was chasing or forcing for naught. I quit passively aggressively shutting down and vowed to let people know what I was feeling instead of retreating when I felt trod-upon.

Then one morning, shortly after this quitting spree, I was busily preparing for a live social media show with my partner, a woman who is traditionally more confident, outspoken, and natural at leading than I am. There, just going about the last-minute, o-crap-my-mic-doesn't work-kind of prep, lo, I had a moment with the Holy Spirit.

I was stressed and irritated and just plain mad about some things on my job, in my friendships, and right there, within our little business relationship. In my head, I heard a voice saying, They don't listen to me. They're not really with me. She could do this show without me. She's not even listening to what I am saying right now.

And that is when I had an answer hit me even harder.

If people do not show up for you... do not retreat.

If people don't show up for you,

Show up for yourself!

My tendency to allow others to purposely, manipulatively, or even unknowingly change my direction was all part of my need for approval. And all that need really served was to falsely fill an empty space in me, one that could only be filled by a belief from the Father to my very soul that He made me to be complete in Him and Him alone.

I had long given other people the power to change my mind simply by not showing support for the things I do or not listening to the things I say. That is not mature or wise behavior, and you know what? I am a grown, wise woman. I have experience. I have value. And I have a voice that doesn't need validation from anyone else.

If I work and rest, love and listen, learn and teach, lead and follow in the rhythm ordained for me by my Father... I will be validated.

And I am.

I will show up where I am needed with what I have to give. But I will not tiptoe across borders into places where I am not invited, and I will not hit heads with clubs and drag people along who do not want to come on my journey.

I will show up for me, because I am validated by Him.

Swerve: Though relationships are treasures, God made us complete in Him.

Consider: Is there a situation that leaves you feeling invalid or not valuable?

Live: 2 Timothy 2:15 tells us to study to show ourselves we are approved of God. Look to His Word to remind yourself how much God loves you and approves of you. This is how we fill ourselves and free ourselves from the sometimes unhealthy need to earn approval from others.

4. Mom-Preneur Life

dealing with wrinkles

"MORTALS MAKE ELABORATE PLANS, BUT GOD HAS THE LAST WORD." PROVERBS 16:1 MSG

"THOSE WRINKLES AIN'T NOTHIN' TO BE SCARED OF, THEY'RE JUST A PRODUCT OF TIME AND TRUE LOVE."
NEIL THRASHER & RONNY SCAIFE

July 9, 2009: The day was fraught with wrinkles. Wrinkles! I had it all figured out, and it all got messy. My dad came over that morning to watch our girls, ages six months and 21 months (aka TWO UNDER TWO!) because the business phone line had been so busy the past few mornings and my usual sitter didn't come until the afternoon. Naturally, the phone was quiet.

When it finally did start ringing, little of it was good. We had THREE exhibitors for our convention cancel, all for unavoidable reasons. I felt so defeated. There were now holes in the schedule and holes in the floor plan, all which had to be addressed on paper and in Real Life.

I was busy setting up radio interviews (as Marketing Director) and making slides with all the artists' names (as Administrative

Assistant), but I stopped and started trying to fix this stuff (as CEO).

I tried to focus, but the phone rang again, and it was Paige (oldest daughter, my afternoon sitter). She got sick at school, like, puke sick, and needed a ride. I went to pick her up and nearly had to throw her out of the car twice on the way home. I think puke in the car might have been the end of all things for me that day.

I scrambled to smooth the wrinkles. I scrambled to find a sitter because, well, I had to run a bank errand and I had to get to my hair appointment (I considered this a work task, because Southern Gospel females must have their hair done). Luckily, our son's girlfriend-now-wife was able to come over for awhile and before I even left, Paige was feeling well enough to help, too.

I planned to cook spaghetti carbonara for dinner, one of our favorites. We'd been eating junk for days and the following week would not improve the situation, so I got Rod to settle the madness of the little ones (Miranda's second day in a row of no nap, Kaity was swan-diving into 'I want Mommy all the time' phase, which I planned to oblige, as soon as the convention was over in two weeks). I started gathering my ingredients and... there was no garlic in the house.

Carbonara requires garlic. Another wrinkle.

I really did not want to drag the kids into a restaurant. They were tired and that ingredient is one that always leads to disaster. So, in true Mother of the Year fashion, I set them in front of Snow White (on VHS!) and vacuumed, because the filthy house was a wrinkle with which I could not contend and also, I was #coping. Rod and I settled on visiting Burrito Station

– quick and easy and somewhat healthful (because, #salsa).

Kaity screamed until the food was served, then flung cheese and lettuce everywhere and repeatedly dipped her little hands in her salsa and the tomato sauce on my enchilada; essentially, tomato sauce was her dinner. Miranda was switching between eating a quesadilla and trying to recline on Paige's lap.

When it was time to leave, they were both screaming for shoes, baba, Mama, and I was nearly screaming, too.

We got the darlings in the bathtub, which was good until Kaity started screaming again, tired, red-eyed, generally pouty. I got her out as soon as Rod was done gently rinsing her, swaddled her in her hooded-Disney Princess towel, and held her in front of the mirror so we could both admire 'the baaaaybeee.'

When I began to lotion and diaper her on the bed, I noticed the wrinkles covering the bottoms of her feet and began to sing a familiar after-bath song, borrowed from Diamond Rio. In a moment, Rod and I switched places/children, and I began singing the song to Miranda, who gave me that look that could win her the Disney castle, the one that says, "Mommy, what you are doing is amazing. You are a magical, super-smart ROCK STAR!"

We eventually settled down... the babies in bed, Rod and I working across from one another at our Ikea double work station. It's all we did in the evening hours for most of the two months leading to our first Southern Gospel music convention, eight hours away, 100 artists, who knows how many audience members. The pace and the juggling made me insane, but the work made me feel like myself again, my pre-family-of-my-own, kick-butt-take-names-project-manager self. I loved what the convention grew into. I loved that for some reason, God chose to use us in that time and place for His reasons. I loved that my best friend and partner in life was my partner in a new career.

Ten years later, as I revisit this story, it is hard for me to imagine living the constant chaos, troubleshooting, and stress of that season for us. We went on to repeat versions of it several more times. And then, we added another child, and having one toddler in our house at that point (and no Burrito Station down the street) was more than enough on its own.

I'd like to tell that younger mama to stock the freezer with chicken nuggets (the good kind) and don't even think about making dinner until after the event. I'd like to tell her that it's okay for the teenagers to pull babysitting and vacuuming duty for a few weeks. I'd like to tell her that one day, those baby girls would retreat to their own corners every night and bathe themselves, no songs necessary. But since I can't, I'll tell you, mama. The plans will go awry, but the important things will get done. Stick to God, surround yourself with a trusted little team, and don't be too quick to iron out the wrinkles. You actually will miss them someday.

Swerve Even when things don't go as planned, it doesn't mean they aren't working out.

Consider Working at home as a mom, with your kids there, is hard. Don't let this surprise you or make you feel like a failure. No one – no one can do everything alone.

Live Look at one aspect of your *boss mom* life that you can delegate. Even small children or surly adolescents can help with household tasks.

5. Chosen Family

disinherited

> "AFTER JOB HAD INTERCEDED FOR HIS FRIENDS, GOD RE-
> STORED HIS FORTUNE—AND THEN DOUBLED IT!"
> JOB 42:10-11 MSG

I have been disinherited by three generations of my family.

It's that simple. It's that awful. I can't go into details, because I still respect the privacy of everyone involved, but grandparents who loved me so well for 25 years of my life, aunts and uncles who were my heroes, cousins who brightened every holiday, and finally, a sibling. All of them, most at the same time and gradually and then suddenly, many years later, said goodbye to me with nary a look back, at least not that I could see.

Oh, how I pondered the reasons why. What if I had said that thing sooner? Or done that thing differently? What if I had lived my life this way, or married that other person, or shared that one belief? Would they still love me? Like me? Want to claim me? Want to know my children? Keep me in their will, or at least, in their contacts list?

To be disinherited will mess with your identity if you don't know who you are. When the first group walked away, I was still a little shaky. I didn't chase them, but I dreamed about them. I didn't beg them, but I missed them. I didn't replace them, but I tried.

When the second exit happened, I was more grounded, less prone to argue, but more hurt. How does this sort of thing happen to a person, twice? What about all we had been through, growing up together? We are our parents' only two children. I still live with so many questions about the "why," but this time, I also live with the peace that I am not the why.

And peace lets us move forward. Oh sure, we carry grief and heartache, but they become a scar rather than a wound or even a scab. My losses remind me, certainly, of how I can make better choices in my relationships, to strive for better understanding.

But they also left empty spaces in my life that only God could fill.

And He did.

I recently got pretty sad on one of those social media holidays –

Sidebar rant: I mean, seriously, I understand Hallmark holidays. Even though we've kind of forsaken greeting cards, the gift industry still does pretty well on Mother's Day, Father's Day, maybe Sweetest Day, but what money do Facebook and Instagram make from Siblings Day/Daughters Day/Puppy Day/etc. etc. etc.?

Anyway... on this recent one, my sweet husband, as he always does, tried to make me feel better, though he feels like an only child himself and came up with very little. In empathy, I told him my heart's truth:

"I have more love in my life than I ever could have deserved."

It doesn't make up for those losses. It means I let God allow me to trade up. For every hole left in my heart, in the life of my family, He brought in people who chose us, who loved us through our worst and celebrated us in our best, who have gathered and stayed – or left and still remember us. We have brothers and sisters, nieces and nephews, more grandparents for our kids than we can count sometimes. We had people pass through who touched us in a season. We have had people think they needed us and it turns out, we needed them.

We have experienced sad losses and the subsequent grief and shame.

We have healed and not given up hope.

We have chosen family – and we have Chosen Family.

Notes on Reconciliation

In the years since I first wrote this, my sibling and I have reached a tentative peace. We are not where we used to be, but we are also not lost to one another, and for that, I am very grateful.

I was also "Facebook reunited" with one of my cousins, who was as sorry as I was for the break in our family and who has been generous in lending me some understanding of why things are the way they are.

Through deeper study of the Bible (see *Resources*), I have come to a deeper understanding of how spiritual oppression and even curses can work in families. Ever heard the phrase, "It ran in the family until it ran into me?" I will always fight for love and peace in the family my husband and I have created. Even so, i know in order to have and maintain it, we all must be submitting to the same God.

I think the older we get, the more clearly we can understand our roots and the supposed "why things are the way they are." I also think... the closer we get to understanding the heart of Jesus, the less it matters. When we love like Him, *He* will protect our hearts.

Swerve Sometimes, we experience loss. This does not mean our hearts will always be empty.

Consider Can you think of a time when God led you to "trade up?" – when He restored or brought relationships into your life that were even greater than what you had in the past?

Live Pray for the ones you have lost. Ask God to bless them, and let them go. Give thanks for the ones He brought, and the ones who will stay.

6. Fitness

transformed

"AND BE NOT CONFORMED TO THIS WORLD: BUT BE YE TRANSFORMED BY THE RENEWING OF YOUR MIND, THAT YE MAY PROVE WHAT IS THAT GOOD, AND ACCEPTABLE, AND PERFECT, WILL OF GOD."
ROMANS 12:2 KJV

Traditionally, I have always hated running. Oh, I joined the "track team" in fifth and sixth grade; the kids made fun of me because I walked faster than I ran. I attempted to run off some weight after my second baby was born. But I quickly returned to finding it loathsome. Until.

A sister-friend of mine who doesn't always believe in herself, and sometimes psyches herself right out of doing things that her absolutely greatness and giftedness would allow her to do, trained all summer for a half-marathon. There was no way I wasn't going to be near the finish line to cheer for her.

I had never gone to a live race. The energy was so positive. I was skipping church to be there (don't worry; the runner I was there for was also one of my pastors), but I was, as it were, getting my praise on.

She did it. She crossed that line.

And so did my other people, at least four others there that I knew. And so did a bunch of other people whose stories I didn't know, but sometimes, I could see just enough on their faces: the man whose spine was bent and looked like he had trouble walking, the woman who was plus sized and smiled so big and beautifully when we cheered for her, the father pushing his grown son in a wheelchair.

It made me say –

Everyone finishing this race has a story. Everyone overcame something to be here.

It's such an easy metaphor for life. The long distance seems so daunting. There is a threat of injury, humiliation, or just plain surrender. We worry about running alone, about not being as fast or efficient or cool as someone else, about not meeting our own expectations, much less those of others. We want to look good. We want to accomplish our personal best. We want to inspire others. We want to finish well.

Right then and there, at that finish line, I had a spiritual moment. I knew it was happening in real time. But I didn't know until a few months later just how deeply I was being changed.

There was a quote I had read just a week or two prior that says,

"One life. Just one. So why aren't we running like we're on fire toward our wildest dreams?"

I wish I knew who said that, so I could hug that person and maybe give her some dark chocolate. It struck me and it stuck with me, and I thought it was metaphorical until the night after the race, when a friend and I registered for our own race and went to the local running store to be fitted for expensive shoes. (Worth. Every. Cent).

My first run was a little awful, a pace of almost 16 minutes per mile (the absolute slowest allowed for most official races). I was winded, my feet hurt, and everything felt heavy. I went almost two miles, but I walked most of it. I felt a little discouraged, but in my mind, I refused to be defeated.

The training schedule for "Couch to Half Marathon" seemed daunting. How would I find the time in my busy mom and work life for all the running involved? And would it even matter? I could barely make it two miles... perhaps I was destined to be a great walker.

Two months later, two-mile outings became a regular thing. Three months later, I ran my first whole mile without walking. Four months later, I was craving runs instead of junk food or naps (most of the time). Five months later, my body was transformed: more endurance, stronger legs, even a tummy finally getting flatter.

What was the difference? Why could I now embrace running and even exercise as a whole when the rest of my entire life, it had been a struggle for me?

I believe it was the renewing of my mind. And friends, that is not just some supernatural outpouring every morning. It is the work of daily reminders: that God created me perfectly and whole, that I am strong, that I don't have to compete with anyone else, that I should drink water, that I don't need a donut to feel good, that one donut once in a while is not a failure in life, that a bad run is better than no run, that my daughters are listening and watching to how I perceive my own body, and I want them to love theirs.

We all have physical limits and shortcomings, and some are

harder to overcome than others. For me, my biggest obstacle was not my extra weight or lack of athleticism: it was my mind telling me for years that I would never be a certain way and definitely never look a certain way. It was my emotions layering on disappointment and guilt and shame. The renewing of my mind brought me confidence, assurance, and love, it allowed me to care for myself as my Creator wants me to, and that is what led to the transformation of self that I desperately wanted and didn't even realize how much I needed.

Swerve: God can help us renew our minds and transform our lives.

Consider: What transformation would make your life better right now?

Live: What daily steps– figurative and physical – can you take to renew how you think about yourself?

7. Gifts of Marriage
steady on

"THE STONE THAT THE BUILDERS REJECTED
HAS NOW BECOME THE CORNERSTONE." PSALM 118:22 NLT

For many years of my adult life, I have lamented and also prayed for something I felt I lacked: emotional steadiness.

I am a passionate person by nature, and my emotions are often rocked even if my outward behavior doesn't reflect that (and sometimes, it very much does). As I grew into my forties, I discovered that some steadiness comes with age and experience. I was learning to temper my emotions and sometimes, truly making choices not to let them come to the surface so easily.

Note: I am not talking about unhealthy forms of emotional repression here. I mean that I don't have to go through three days of angst over someone not responding to a text or liking a Facebook post, nor do I have to experience three days of sorrow over the death of a fictional character.

One night, sitting in a group of women, I heard several stories of marriages with shaky ground and big issues: Financial strife. Lack of intimacy. Failure to work together. Misunderstanding. Absence of communication, affection, and partnership. I listened and doled out advice where I could, and on the way home, received a word of my own:

You've never wanted to leave.

This was important, you guys. Not because my marriage is "better than that one" *or that one*. But because God showed me *why* my marriage is a little different from some of the ones around me, and also that there *is* a space in my life where I am steady.

See, Rod and I had a whole lot of shaky ground covered by the time we got married. Like, whenever social media circulates those "How did you and your husband meet?" and "Where was your first date?" kind of things, I still have to shy away. Our foundation was inherently fragile, because we began with our own guilt and shame, with family and friends jumping ship, and with a *love conquers all* mindset that was not necessarily humble, but probably responsible for carrying us through those rough early years.

We fought to defy all the statistical odds that were against us from the beginning. We overcame medical reports that said we'd never have children together. And then we overcame financial hardship after a move halfway across the country culminated in the depletion of our savings, the destruction of our credit, and months of very unexpected unemployment.

We helped each other overcome our pasts: troubled relationships and walls built around our hearts as a result. I don't know if that is *why*, but I do know that not once, not in an inkling of doubt over his love or a moment of fury over any small or big thing, have I ever considered us not being together. I've never played "What if I left?" inside my head. I've never pondered what I would do if *he* left. I've never even contemplated that he might.

There is no exit strategy built into our marriage, no secret slush fund just in case, no plan B. And *that* is the steadiness that has existed in my life since we got married in 2003.

It's just like our God, my friends, to take a concept we yearn to master (steadiness) and take a piece of our lives that others might not understand (a marriage after adultery), and use them, fuse them together, to create something rock solid.

My cornerstone, my adult life, my redemption story began with my marriage. It's not a secret to success or a guarantee of longevity, but it is a daily inspiration, gift, and testimony.

God gives us people and relationships to fill the empty spaces. It is how He loves.

Swerve: Sometimes we think we are missing something that is right in front of us.

Consider: What has your closest relationship added to your life?

Live: Tell your significant other – be it your spouse, your parent, your best friend – exactly what spaces your relationship has filled for you.

8. New Dreams

this is who you are

"IF RACING AGAINST MERE MEN MAKES YOU TIRED, HOW WILL YOU RACE AGAINST HORSES?" JEREMIAH 12:5 NLT

A dear friend of mine has known numerous and major upheavals in his ministry years. In the past several, the declining health of several family members and the betrayal of a few close friends has added heaps of stress.

Though all of that seems like a shaky foundation on which to build a new dream, he has. In the midst of evidence that would suggest a time to doubt and be timid, he instead planted his flag on a foundation of "GO BIG OR GO HOME." In the time frame of less than four months, he and his team formed an internationally-reaching organization, branded it, put a board in place, and held its first annual conference.

Oh, I get this. Not so long ago, my husband and I created a business venture with a partner who duped and stole from us. We continued on for two more years and some modicum of success before letting it go to move to the next dream. That one included moving our family and our lives halfway across the country, for a venture that ultimately (rather, quickly, really) completely flopped, leaving us indebted, nearly bankrupt, and quite alone in what felt like a foreign land.

Sometimes our circumstances flash red, "Do not proceed. Dead end. Turn the heck around."

Sometimes, our past experiences would have us afraid to try anything new.

But those failures and knock-downs are just street signs on the path to our greatest victories. They are flashing lights that slow us down enough to learn our lessons and refuel, and they redirect us to better routes that lead to better places.

On the morning of my friend's launch, I was pondering the keynote message he was set to give, inspired by Jeremiah's words. And I, in the midst of my own journey to running a half marathon, was inspired to send him this:

> *This is who you are. It's what you've been doing since I've known you. And I am learning about running firsthand and literally. Running is life-giving, endurance-building, dream-inspiring. It also brings with it traffic to dodge, holes and poop to step in, fatigue, people who don't understand or even resent you for it, big hills upward and victories. IT'S ALL OKAY. There is beauty surrounding these horses even when they don't see it. They're just following the voice inside them that says, "Go this way." I am so proud of you for going this way. I am honored to be a part of saddling horses and blazing trails.*

Everyone fails sometimes. Even Jesus, in His humanity, did

not always see the desired results of His efforts in ministry or relationship (see: Judas Iscariot). The important part of failure is not that we experience it, but rather, how we rebound from it. Don't stay down. Get back on the horse, keep dreaming your dreams, run a new race.

Swerve: Often what we thought was a destination for us is more of a fork in the road, directing us to something better than we imagined.

Consider: You are not alone in failure. Everyone experiences it. What about your failures can make you wiser and stronger?

Live: Is there someone around you who is experiencing fear beset by past or current disappointments? Encourage that person in a specific, personal way.

Miscarriage Part 1

laughing again

"HE WILL ONCE AGAIN FILL YOUR MOUTH WITH LAUGHTER AND YOUR LIPS WITH SHOUTS OF JOY." JOB 8:21 NLT

At age 37, three weeks after joyfully and wholeheartedly accepting a *very* surprise pregnancy, I checked "miscarriage" off the bucket list of nightmares I hoped never to face. It was the worst kind of surprise, to go in excitedly for a first doctor visit only to be told "There is no heartbeat." It knocked us down hard. But we survived.

Miscarriage is horrible for all sorts of reasons. It is a death of a person. It is the death of so many hopes. It is the death of a family make-up and all the dreams of the future that go with it. And whether it happens in your first pregnancy or like mine, in your third, it is the death of any innocence around pregnancy. Miscarriage really exists. Babies are really stolen from our lives before they ever see the sun. It is unnatural and cruel and impossible to understand unless you've been through it.

My first miscarriage brought me to a place of grief I had never experienced before, but because there was grief around me, including that of my six-and-seven-year-old-daughters, and because there was also *life* around me – our oldest son and his wife of six weeks were newly pregnant, I kept grief at bay and outwardly, became a much more stoic person than my family and friends were used to seeing.

I remember the day I found my laughter again. It was three or four weeks after my D&C. We were lounging in bed on a Saturday morning, waiting for the girls to come and jump on us. They did. And for some reason, I grabbed my iPhone and turned on the Pharrell song "Happy." (You so know the one). Then I started lip syncing. And dancing. Rod was watching me with the light in his eyes you can only have for the person you adore when she is being completely odd.

And I cracked up. And I couldn't stop.

That was the day I found myself again. Even though when I look back at my early life, I see a thread of melancholy, the real truth that has arisen as I have "found myself" in adulthood is that I am a joyful person. I smile. I laugh. I embrace happiness. Having a family of my own, becoming a mama, helped me to see that and be that. And while losing a child could have been the thing that changed it (as indeed, it *did* change me to my core), I refuse to let it.

> Death doesn't win.
> Fear doesn't win.

Joy, love, laughter… it will, it must conquer the sad things in life. It will give us wings.

It did for this time. Three months later, in the spirit of twofold blessings and almost three months to the day we lost our baby, we found out we would be having another. I will never forget the glory that filled the room when we saw his heart beating and his miraculous little arms waving.

And I laughed...

Swerve: Life can rob us of circumstances, but God's spiritual gifts, like JOY, cannot be taken from us.

Consider: What has stolen your joy?

Live: Ask God to restore your joy. It is not too much to ask; it is a gift He freely gave through His Holy Spirit and a manifestation He will not withhold from you. Give yourself permission to receive it.

10. Submission

a food rebel surrenders

"Why do you spend money for what is not bread,
And your wages for what does not satisfy?
Listen carefully to Me, and eat what is good,
And delight yourself in abundance." Isaiah 55:2 KJV

"Submit yourselves therefore to God. Resist the
devil, and he will flee from you." James 4:7

A year after I started running, I would occasionally still get two specific comments:
1. "How much weight have you lost?"
2. "When are you due?"

The former was difficult because in spite of running miles and miles and miles, exercising and sweating more than ever in my life and certainly turning some of my body fat into muscle, I had not lost any discernible weight at all.

The latter was humiliating because my extra weight was most definitely concentrated in my waistline, and it wasn't a stretch at all to assume I was pregnant.

Two years after I started running, I trained for my first marathon. If you have never done this, there are a few things you might not know. One is that when you are running 30-40 miles a week, you are hungry a whole bunch of the time – especially if you don't eat the right things. The other is that, sort of like with pregnancy, so many parts of your body are affected in random, mysterious ways. For me, there was a lot of calf tightness that led to some foot problems (it's all connected), some random swelling in one ankle, and a whole bunch of digestive issues.

Two-and-a-half years after I started running, I had brunch with the same friend who crossed a half-marathon finish line and inspired me to run. Without prompting, she started telling me about a medical weight loss program that she and her husband and mutual friends of ours had used. It sounded hard core, and expensive, and very, very intriguing. I called and made an appointment with that doctor on my way back from that brunch.

A few days later, my pastor preached a sermon on rebelliousness and submission. I was at my normal station, in the production booth, overseeing the livestream and multimedia aspects of the service. And I could not stop crying. Long removed from the wild days of my early 20s, I considered myself a fairly compliant person when it comes to faith and Jesus. But as my pastor's message went on, I looked into the proverbial mirror and saw two areas of my life that were swathed in rebelliousness: one was my parenting (that's a story for another time), another was my diet.

I mean diet, not dieting. I mean everything that I consume. I love food: cooking it, tasting it, watching shows about it, reading about it, writing about it, ordering it. But I no longer have the metabolism that allowed my 5'2 frame to regularly consume nachos and chocolate milk (as I did every day of high school) and stay slender, or even proportioned. I had been eating like I was at a carnival for years, gone through eight abdominal surgeries and five pregnancies, and was over 40... and that had added up to baggage that I could not outrun and that was becoming too physically and emotionally heavy to carry.

> *I went to my appointment just a few days later determined to submit my taste buds, appetite, and weight to the Lord.*

It had taken me a lot of discipline to train for that marathon while working two jobs and raising three kids; what could stop me from finally losing weight if I dedicated myself just the same? On the way to that doctor visit, I played "I Surrender All" on repeat and sang along in my car. And though somewhat intimidated by the specifics of the weight loss regimen I was prescribed, I went home and wrote in lipstick on my mirror. This time, I didn't write a target time for an upcoming big race. Instead, I wrote a daily calorie goal I was going to try to meet for 30 days.

As I write this, I am on day 28. I am over 16 pounds lighter. (We are on vacation, and I did not bring a scale!) While my family ate burgers and fries tonight, I ate a salad with grilled chicken and lemon juice. Yesterday, we went to The Cheesecake Factory, and I didn't have cheesecake! I brought a low-carb hard cider with me on this trip and haven't touched it. When my family offers some good-natured-and-intended sympathy over these small sacrifices that feel like big victories, I am reminded anew of the things my Father has taught me during this season of... well, pretty much fasting:

1. I am not the same person who gained all this weight. She was depressed, insecure, searching. I am a new creature, who understands grace, has confidence through Him who strengthens me, and is living an abundant life.

2. *I am not fulfilled by food, but by love.*

3. Food is a fuel for my body; the goal for my body is to be strong, healthy, and energetic.

4. Food can be satisfying without being junk.

5. Occasional junk is okay, eventually, after I am finished surrendering to this process.

6. No matter what I weigh or look like, Jesus loves me, and I have been made worthy of that love.

7. Running is a love for me in and of itself, not a means for me to eat without intention or control.

8. Good times and rewards do not have to revolve around treats.

I am only halfway to my weight loss goal and a long way from "keeping it off." But the changes in me have been drastic. There are the physical ones, which start with the scale and include the size adjusters I need for my wedding rings to keep them from flying off, the fact that my shirts and pants and even some shoes are too big, the random swelling I thought was from running disappearing, my increased stamina, and most dramatically, what I see when I look in the mirror or a photograph of me.

There are also mental and emotional changes. I have examined how food's importance became skewed to me and what I will need to do to keep it in its proper perspective without medical assistance. Surrendering all will need to be a continual process, long after my weight loss goal, by the grace of God, is met.

I think sometimes we are afraid that if we give something up, we automatically have less and are less. I know we are afraid of giving up control of the things that comfort us. All this process is showing me is that submitting to God and His best for me is the safest and most satisfying state in which I can be. As my physical mass decreases, so does my doubt and shame and the weight of anxiety and self-consciousness. As I continually submit my desires to God, just like always, He is faithful to give me new desires and fulfill each one.

Swerve: Rebelliousness doesn't just look like drug addictions or breaking the law. Any act that goes against God's best for us or how Holy Spirit is leading us is one of rebellion.

Consider: Is there a desire, a hobby, a method, a relationship, or some other area that you have held on though you hear God telling you "no"?

Live: Name this area to God. Ask Him to help you surrender. And then, through His help, do it! He will fill your empty places!

11. Fitting In

a lesson from my daughter

"ALL KINDS OF THINGS ARE HANDED OUT BY THE SPIRIT, AND TO ALL KINDS OF PEOPLE! THE VARIETY IS WONDERFUL... ALL THESE GIFTS HAVE A COMMON ORIGIN, BUT ARE HANDED OUT ONE BY ONE BY THE ONE SPIRIT OF GOD. HE DECIDES WHO GETS WHAT, AND WHEN."
FROM 1 CORINTHIANS 12, MSG

She runs outside with the other girls, excitedly whooping and ready for adventure. They're all cute as buttons, pictures of what little girls look like in their homemade t-shirts and bare feet, or dress up clothes and funny socks.

I look at the window just minutes later, and she is there, alone, playing on the climbing wall, having an adventure with herself.

It's taken awhile, but I've learned that these are not sad adventures, and this is not a lonely child. Sometimes, most times, she does not fit in. She is the one with the "thing" that I can't quite put my finger on, the thing that isn't a diagnosis or a label. She is going to dress her way, imagine her way, and demand her way. She is going to challenge me, and she is going to be challenged.

She is mighty. She is a leader. And she is a child. And that last one sometimes trumps the first two, and the brave warrior comes crashing down, with angry accusations and heart-wrenching tears that break her mama's heart, because I never wanted my five-year-old to feel that level of fear, of uncertainty, of rejection, of humiliation, or frankly, of intensity.

On church day, a friend comes to me. She knows me pretty well by now, and she embraces me as she tells me what she feels God has shown her. It's confirmation, so I know it's true. One daughter, she says, is just like her daddy. And this one, she is like you.

'God is showing you what you were like, so you can see... so you can see...'

Like me? This five-year-old with bravery that I envy? With confidence that I long for? With coolness that I strive for? She is me? Did I leave others in awe? Did I leave my parents in manic states of amusement and frustration and utter bewilderment at my brilliance? Surely not.

But now, colored with perspective, I watch her today. I remember the stories I began to write at age six, excited ramblings and detailed imaginings. I remember how my heart reached out for others, wanted to be like them, but could never quite change enough to fit. I know that looking back at the girl I was...age six, age nine, age 12, age 18... age 35, that I was beautiful, but I didn't see it, so I tried to be something else, anything else.

I look in the mirror and see the same blue eyes and pale skin as our youngest daughter, the one who does not look at all like her three older siblings, (who've captured their daddy's little bit of Cherokee blood, deep brown eyes, and great ability to tan), the one whose flowing blond mane calls to mind "Irish Lass" or "Tinkerbell" until people realize it's more like "Buzz Lightyear" or "Thor." Can I have the same care, the same grace, for my own reflection as I have for my baby girl? Can I accept, even celebrate, that those uncategorizable differences my Father gave to me make me special and fun and even great? Can I accept the beauty that others insist is there, in spite of the wiry grays and the extra pounds and general feelings of awkwardness? Can I apply the lesson that adventures of my own making, taken alone, are acceptable and even enough, if they are what I am meant to have?

ꙫ

I look outside again, just after writing those words, and see the girls have regrouped. They run off again, except now one has stayed behind with my warrior, swinging on a tire just feet away, companionable but separate. Companionable but separate: kind of like my husband, reading across the room but smiling knowingly at me on the occasions I look up... or my Dad, who sometimes smirks and shakes his head at my "Kelly-ness"... or those friends, some 1000 miles away and some at the next desk, who know my fake smile from my real one (even on Facebook) and when to call me on it.

We were not made to be just like everyone else.

We were not made always to fit in the crowd, but sometimes to get lost in it, and sometimes run circles around it. She will be okay, and so will I. And if this resounds in your spirit, so will you.

Swerve: We were made to be unique, not to fit in.

Consider: Have you ever noticed something about your child that makes you crazy, and realized you have the same trait?

Live: Be intentional about cultivating your child's extremes. Compliment, challenge, talk it out, affirm.

12. Insecurity

just for a second

> "GOD'S SPIRIT TOUCHES OUR SPIRITS AND CONFIRMS WHO WE REALLY ARE. WE KNOW WHO HE IS, AND WE KNOW WHO WE ARE: FATHER AND CHILDREN. AND WE KNOW WE ARE GOING TO GET WHAT'S COMING TO US—AN UNBELIEVABLE INHERITANCE!" – ROMANS 8:16, MSG

It was a beautiful moment, joy mixed with welcome, nostalgia mixed hope, love mixed with... more love.

I held a new life in my arms after a deep anticipation to do that very thing, to look into that tiny face, to behold that new-life smell, to breathe in the promise that a living being, still so pure, holds for us all.

And I almost let it get ruined by my own doubt, my own insecurity, my own need to feel needed.

I made an assumption, inwardly for weeks and out loud in that moment, about my role in that child's life. I was wrong about the label, and I was wrong about the timing. I made it awkward for the baby's mom, for the mutual friends around us, and certainly for myself.

Thankfully, my friends were close, and their grace was sufficient. Still, some time shortly after that moment, I was crying to my husband.

"*Why am I never quite good enough? Why am I always second choice?*"

He did what any good husband does, one who knows his wife better than anyone else, one which buttons are necessary, correct, or okay to push at any given time.

He laughed at me.

He said something like, **"You are exactly where you want to be right now. Quit worrying."**

But I didn't stop worrying.

Seven years later, I was having the same conversation. This time with my boss, telling him the same story, because after all, I am his second assistant.

He didn't give me that label. I did.

He also laughed at me, and said,

"You aren't anyone's second choice. They were all just too stupid to wait for you."

Ha, ha, ha. LOL...

Second born, second wife, second assistant, second place, second choice. I can make it all make sense in my head. I can focus so myopically on what I was not chosen for, when I am not a priority, that I push aside all the instances in which I am first:

    - to my husband, over just about anything.
    - to my kids when they have big news, a school project, a major conflict with one another, a major need at Target,

Starbucks, Amazon, or any bookstore...

- to my sister-friends when they have life decisions to make, funny observations about newly binge-watched shows, or serious decisions to make about career/family/geography/new glasses

- to my co-workers when they need to know their own passwords (LOL again)

But more importantly, *most importantly*, God does not look at me as a second place at all. Reread the scripture above: We are *joint heirs* with Jesus Christ – children of God, created in His image!

If the God of the Universe thinks I am all that, what does it matter if I am chosen last for the softball team in fifth grade gym class, passed over as godmother or maid of honor, relegated to the co- or assistant, or any thousand grown-up versions of the same thing?

It shouldn't. It still does to me most of the time, but it shouldn't. And I am working on that.

If you continue reading on in Romans 8, one of my very favorite passages of the Bible, there are many promises to God's kids. But there are a lot of responsibilities given to us as well~

WE GO THROUGH EXACTLY WHAT CHRIST GOES THROUGH. IF WE GO THROUGH THE HARD TIMES WITH HIM, THEN WE'RE CERTAINLY GOING TO GO THROUGH THE GOOD TIMES WITH HIM! – ROMANS 8:17, THE MESSAGE

We have to take our licks. We have to lose sometimes. We can't get everything we want. We cannot achieve perfection. But this promise says we get to go through all of it – good and bad – with God. WITH Him.

Just for a second, this second-born-syndrome girl is going to dwell on that. And I'm going to keep praying it gets etched in my heart and mind. I'm nothing but first place to my Father, and neither are you.

Swerve: Even when we do not receive the accolades our emotions want, we can be secure in our very souls that God loves us completely.

Consider: We cannot be everyone's favorite. But we each can be God's favorite. Don't you just love His mysterious ways?

Live: Next time you feel that nagging voice in your head say you are not enough, affirm God's love to yourself. Sing "Jesus Loves Me" right out loud. Write your favorite Psalm in your journal (My favorite is 103). Or simply declare out loud that you are His. The voice of Holy Spirit is happy to speak louder than the voices of your insecurities, if only you will listen.

13. Miracles

the end of infertility

"FOR I KNOW THE THOUGHTS THAT I THINK TOWARD YOU, SAITH THE LORD, THOUGHTS OF PEACE, AND NOT OF EVIL, TO GIVE YOU AN EXPECTED END." JEREMIAH 29:11 KJV

Written April 12, 2006, in the real-time waiting of a very specific pregnancy test.

I became a Christian – a real choice to become a Christian, when I was seven years old. The sect of Christianity I practice emphasizes a personal relationship with Christ... prayer, love, dependency, communion. Not rituals, but relationship.

I've had a roller coaster relationship with God. I've always loved Him, always believed... but often strayed. Neglected my faith. Neglected the relationship. Made stupid decisions that made me a hypocrite because they went against the things I believed. This cycle went on and on. I think it nearly killed me a few times.

And fast forward... mid-20s. Tumultuous life? Gone. Suddenly: peace. I am married and a stepmom. And then... WORST NIGHTMARE: INFERTILITY. I carried on, finish college, started my dream career, made tentative adoption plans, watched my brother get married, felt like my family was all at peace, fa la la la la.

Before, peace has always alluded me. But somewhere, even in my devastating infertility diagnosis, it became mine. I quit fighting God about things and stopped feeling punished by Him for mistakes I made. I started to believe the verses, like the one above, that I had clung to all these years – but never really took to my own heart. And others, like these:

"Sing, O barren, thou that didst not bear; break forth into singing, and cry aloud, thou that didst not travail with child: for more are the children of the desolate than the children of the married wife, saith the Lord... Fear not; for thou shalt not be ashamed: neither be thou confounded; for thou shalt not be put to shame: for thou shalt forget the shame of thy youth, and shalt not remember the reproach of thy widowhood any more... For thy Maker is thine husband; the Lord of hosts is his name; and thy Redeemer the Holy One of Israel; The God of the whole earth shall he be called. For the Lord hath called thee as a woman forsaken and grieved in spirit, and a wife of youth, when thou wast refused, saith thy God. For a small moment have I forsaken thee; but with great mercies will I gather thee. In a little wrath I hid my face from thee for a moment; but with everlasting kindness will I have mercy on thee, saith the Lord thy Redeemer." Isaiah 54: 1, 4-8 KJV

"Remember ye not the former things, neither consider the things of old. Behold, I will do a new thing; now it shall spring forth; shall ye not know it? I will even make a way in the wilderness, and rivers in the desert." Isaiah 43: 19 KJV

"Delight thyself also in the Lord: and he shall give thee

the desires of thine heart. Commit thy way unto the Lord; trust also in him; and he shall bring it to pass." Psalm 37: 4 KJV

"For the Lord God is a sun and shield: the Lord will give grace and glory: no good thing will he withhold from them that walk uprightly." Psalm 84:11 KJV

Over the course of several weeks, my belief evolved – as did the slow, evolving belief that I am pregnant, has been about more than believing I am pregnant. I mean, the doctor said, **"LESS THAN ONE PERCENT CHANCE OF GETTING PREGNANT NATURALLY (AND WE DON'T SAY ZERO BECAUSE WE NEVER SAY ZERO")**. That is what he said. He also said in vitro was a slim to nil chance for us. Why shouldn't I have a hard time believing that I'm pregnant now? People giggle a little when I say I missed my March period and haven't taken a test yet. They don't get it. It is MEDICALLY almost IMPOSSIBLE for me to get pregnant.

Thankfully:

"For with God nothing shall be impossible." Luke 1:37 KJV

And that is the real miracle for me, folks. I finally believe not only in God, not only in His love and grace, but in His desire for me to experience that love and grace. I know He has forgiven me long ago, has blessed me and led me to wonderful people and opportunities, but I always felt this baby miracle was beyond me. I believed God could do it, would do it for other people, but that probably there was a reason why it wouldn't happen for me, and I also, of course, thought I knew the reasons.

I have been teaching four of my classes about hubris: the Greek term for pride humans feel that makes them arrogant, makes them forget that they have limitations the gods do not. How dare I decide I know better than God does what He should and shouldn't, would and wouldn't, give to me? He is the creator of the universe; I am the creator of amateur stories.

And now, I am a believer in His love for me.

After 22 years of saying it, I believe it. Today, right now, butterflies in my stomach, I believe it.

So it doesn't matter so much what the little pee stick says in a little while. I hope with all my heart and soul that it tells me I am giving a baby to the world, that I get to be a mommy. But if it does not, I will not be crushed or devastated. The last three weeks have brought me to an amazing place in my heart and in my faith. I have seen my friends and people who barely know me feel inspired by the very idea that this could happen. That is God. That is His power and His love. And whether there is a baby growing in me right now or not, the glory for it all is His.

Amen.

Swerve: Miracles still happen. They can still happen in our own stories.

Consider: What miracle have you witnessed in your life? Are you currently in need of a miracle?

Live: Celebrate the miracles around you, whether they are "yours" or not. Share those stories. Encourage yourself and others with those words. God loves us all equally, and He wants us to be whole.

14.
Helplessness

foster families and failed fixes

"BEFORE I SHAPED YOU IN THE WOMB, I KNEW ALL ABOUT YOU. BEFORE YOU SAW THE LIGHT OF DAY, I HAD HOLY PLANS FOR YOU..." JEREMIAH 1:5 MSG

Sometimes, we cannot fix it. "It" can be a lot of things, but becoming a foster aunt opened my eyes to my own helplessness in a brand-new way.

A few years ago, one of my closest friends – in fact, the closest person I have to a sister – and her husband, became foster parents. My friend never bore her own children and is one of those people who simply exudes the heart of a mother. The road to certification was long and complicated, but finally, they received their first placement: an adolescent girl we will call Charlotte, seemingly open to friends and a new start, sweet, conversational, even bearing a bit of a physical resemblance to her new foster mom.

For two years, life with Charlotte was a roller coaster. She drew very close to my own daughters and very close to her foster mom. She was part of our family, holding a place in so many chapters of our lives. But she was troubled. We have no idea the causes of all the behaviors she displayed, and my friends fought tooth and nail to get her all the help it was determined she needed. Counseling, medication, therapy, school modifications, dance class, rewards, carefully-legislated punishments: everything that can be tried in the confines of foster families was attempted over and over.

My friends were out of town on a short and needed getaway when Charlotte's behaviors began to carry physical threats to other members of their household. For the second time in two years, they had to let her go, to allow her to move on to alternate care.

In the meantime, while they were away, Charlotte came to spend two days with us. I knew what was going to happen in her life at that point. She did not. My girls did not. Though my husband did, our house is hardly soundproof, so we couldn't talk about it.

I carried it. For those two days and nights, I carried one of the most tenuous broken hearts I have ever nursed. To look at Charlotte was to see an ordinary kid, so much like my own in her clothing, her interests, even her personality. I had never witnessed the destructive behavior that was causing so much upheaval in her young life. It was hard to imagine. But I did see the havoc, stress, and heartache it wreaked in the lives of my friends and the rest of their family. This only added to my own sorrow.

I knew this would be our last chance to give to Charlotte. Though there was no timeline for her departure from the family, she would likely not be allowed to spend the night or even have many recreational gatherings with us prior to moving to her next home. The still, small voice of the Holy Spirit inside me was not subtle or quiet during this time. It simply said, "Love her. Love her lots. Don't hold back."

So we loved.

There were cookies baked and movies watched and even plans discussed (it was almost Christmastime). At church that Sunday, she even asked me to pray with her, for her own biological sister. She had no idea that while I prayed and put my arm around her and cried rather uninhibitedly, I was asking God for all the things we all wanted for her: Healing. Peace. Good decisions. Changed behavior. Safety. The perfect forever home.

Occasionally, this being a small town, we hear a tidbit about how Charlotte is doing. Sometimes the news is not encouraging. It's possible my daughter will attend the same school as her again, and perhaps we will have another line into her life. I hold that idea tenuously as well – because my heart went so completely to this child, I almost convinced myself that love was enough, that if she was gathered in our arms and our community, we could fix everything for her.

And hardest to admit, I also convinced myself that maybe even if my friends couldn't continue raising her, maybe my husband and I somehow could.

These were all desperate hopes, a result of keeping my eyes in the wrong place. Because though the facts in front of me say that Charlotte is a little girl failed by her birth parents and lost in a system, the truth is one our community gave to her from the beginning: From the time she was conceived, she belonged to God. No matter what she sees, hears, experiences, she belongs to Him. He loves her more than any of us ever could. He is capable of keeping her safe and making her whole: if she will choose His freedom over her fear, faith in Him over what she sees and feels.

On the outskirts of the foster care system, the plight of these misplaced children devastates me on a continual basis. Our household is not eligible for fostering, and to be honest, we are not sure we'd be equipped. We continue to support our friends and other foster families through local organizations. The first letter I ever wrote to a member of congress was to protect the rights of foster children. But it isn't enough. It is not a fix.

Only God can fix it.

Swerve: No matter how deeply we might love people, God created them and loves them even more.

Consider: What situations make us feel helpless? What we can we do to lessen that feeling?

Live: Helplessness is a byproduct of fear. Fear can only be conquered by faith. Compile your own list of scriptures or journal a few of your past victorious experiences. Read through these and mediate on them when you feel helpless or heartbroken in your circumstances.

Note: Through the power of social media, Charlotte remains intermittently connected to our lives. Say a prayer for her and for all those kids and families who need love, peace, and a home.

15. Friendship

the best kind of friends

> "SINCE GOD CHOSE YOU TO BE THE HOLY PEOPLE HE LOVES, YOU MUST CLOTHE YOURSELVES WITH TENDERHEARTED MERCY, KINDNESS, HUMILITY, GENTLENESS, AND PATIENCE. MAKE ALLOWANCE FOR EACH OTHER'S FAULTS, AND FORGIVE ANYONE WHO OFFENDS YOU. REMEMBER, THE LORD FORGAVE YOU, SO YOU MUST FORGIVE OTHERS. ABOVE ALL, CLOTHE YOURSELVES WITH LOVE, WHICH BINDS US ALL TOGETHER IN PERFECT HARMONY." COLOSSIANS 3:12-14 NLT

> "A BOWL OF VEGETABLES WITH SOMEONE YOU LOVE IS BETTER THAN STEAK WITH SOMEONE YOU HATE."
> PROVERBS 5:17 NLT

For most of my life, I felt like I didn't have that quintessential group of friends that we saw so gloriously portrayed on *Beverly Hills, 90210*, and *Different World* and well, *Friends*. As I look back now, I can clearly see that I *always* had friends, and usually, a good number of them.

But what I had failed to see in my early years, and unfortunately, didn't learn until after those emerging adult years, was that really, *no friend* is meant to be the be all, end all, BFF. When we are growing up, we change too much to fill that role. When we are grown, we are responsible for too much to fill that role. God had a perfect design in mind: He is the best friend we need, and He fills our lives with the best *kind* of friends.

The best kinds of friends, it turns out, serve different roles in our lives, and they also serve for differing periods of time. Oh, that was the hardest lesson in friendship for me so far. I remember when we moved to a new house, when my babies were aged one, seven, and eight. We downsized by several rooms and hundreds of square feet, and I purged about one-third of our possessions. One hot, humid, July afternoon (because our South Carolina-based family can only move when it's 120 degrees outside), I was standing over a garbage bin going through three huge bags filled with stuffed animals – and I could recall who gave each one and on what occasion.

But I still had to throw those plush little suckers away.

Letting friendships go can be painful, and the heartbreak can be lasting, but losing friends is *inevitable*. So rather than stewing in bitterness or regret over who could not or would not be what I wanted, I am learning to think of friends like those stuffed animals, in a way. I hugged you tight. You brought me joy. And either I outgrew you or you had a different place to go. And occasionally, like that cardboard-stiff Sponge Bob our oldest son won at a carnival, you probably were never meant for me in the first place.

When we allow God to fill the spaces of our hearts, and this is important, when we let Him guide us to the relationships we are *supposed* to have...

(even if they're not with the cool kids, or the Pinterest moms, or the trendy church leaders)

... the friends we have will be *enough*.

The ups and downs of the 30s decade, of settling into our own lives with our own kids and careers and all kinds of grown-up stuff often shows us the friends we are supposed to have. When I was the lonely new girl in town, one friend whom I don't have any more gave me this simple advice, and it proved to be true: *Let friendships come to you.*

Ask God to open your eyes to them. He is your best friend and won't let you down.

Blessed are the friends~
>who love up close and those who love from afar.
>who love in bold declarations and those who love in quiet prayers.
>who love in daily text messages and those who love in annual visits.
>who love in tough honesty and those who love in flowery greeting cards.

Blessed are the friends~
>who show up at the hospital and those who wish they could.
>who bring gluten free snacks or cheese for your chili or their empty stomach to your refrigerator.
>who love your children and your parents.
>who joke about your failures and celebrate your victories.
>who don't want you to change your 708 phone number even though they have no idea what it is.
>who share recipes, request recipes, and alter recipes.
>who remember your important details and signature stories.

Swerve

Blessed are the friends~
    you've known since grade school
    you haven't seen since high school
    you have never met in person
    you are just now finally getting to know.

Blessed are the friends~
    who give what you need
    and who receive what you give.

Blessed are the friends~
    who love backstage, when you need the encouragement,
    who love in the spotlight, because we learn from them,
    who love all the time... who are needed, and treasured,
    more than words can say.

Swerve: The way a friendship ends does not take away any lessons, benefits, or happy memories gained from the time it existed.

Consider: Are you chasing what you think friendship should look like, or loving whom God is putting in your circle?

Live: Write a goodbye letter to a friend you have lost – even if you never send it, and pray for God to make your heart open for the friends you are meant to have.

16. Miscarriage Part 2

faith for life

"THE SPIRIT OF GOD HAS MADE ME,
AND THE BREATH OF THE ALMIGHTY GIVES ME LIFE."
JOB 33:4

Let put this disclaimer out there: I cannot even pretend to touch the subject of grief. It's big and it's personal, and from my standpoint, it suffers even more by comparison. In these past few years, I have had friends who lost an infant, lost a young child, lost a young adult child, lost a husband, lost mothers and fathers. All these losses blow my mind and my heart. I can't speak to them. I can only speak to *my* deepest grief thus far...

Shortly after my first miscarriage, I was part of a conversation about a mutual friend who was pregnant. The theme of the conversation was fear. It was, "Yikes. That news is out there early... what if something bad happens?"

It was a reference I understood. When I first confirmed I was pregnant with Miranda (April 12, 2006 lives in infamy for me!), I had absolutely no intention of waiting to share the news. In my spirit of storytelling, I'd certainly shared my monthly disappointments of "no pregnancy this time" with people (and this was Before Facebook). Why wouldn't I share the good news? That whole wait until the *second trimester* thing was far from my mind.

My husband told me later how worried he had been. Miranda was my first pregnancy after a diagnosis of infertility. She was my first pregnancy ever. Chances were good (about 20 percent) that we'd have a miscarriage. And in a moment of celebration at Aurelio's Pizza, a moment I told few people about, I went to the bathroom and found I was spotting. At my first doctor's appointment, after I had taken 1-2-3-4-5-6-SEVEN tests at home, there was a faint enough line to cause the doctor to put me through a blood test and a 24-hour wait before she'd even acquiesce that I was, in fact, pregnant.

You know what I did after we left that doctor appointment? We went to Babies R Us and made a registry.

This wasn't because I was not scared. If I paused to think about it, I would have lost my mind with doubt and terror.

But I am a story gal – I have a pretty large and intense imagination. Because of this, I am at times forced to compartmentalize. It is all too easy for me to vividly imagine the worst, to put myself in different shoes. I have to selectively ignore possibilities sometimes. It's not me being naive; it's rescuing me from me.

As the story goes, the blood test was positive, the spotting was nothing, and Miranda Rose arrived in all her glory 7 months later (ironically, by the time I knew I was pregnant, I was almost in my second trimester).

Perhaps that is why a miscarriage eight years later knocked me down so hard. Miscarriages, in my vague frame of reference at that time, happened to young women, first-timers, people in accidents... not to older moms with previous perfect pregnancies. The idea of pregnancy number three resolving that way was not something I had considered for one single second.

So what do you do when you get pregnant after that?

Let me back up. David James, the baby we lost, was not planned. He was a huge, amazing surprise. Jack, however, is the only baby we ever "tried for" and got. With Miranda, I did not think I could get pregnant. With Kaity, who was conceived when Miranda was but six months old, I was mentally in a place of "it happened once but it probably won't happen again." (Irony is the story of my life/all life). With Jack, there were calendars... well, apps, because it was 2014. In fact, I know the day he was made (I'm not gonna write about it here, but if you ask me, I will tell you something about Disney World and pixie dust...)

※

On the Sunday before Memorial Day in 2014, a new friend of mine announced on Facebook that she was pregnant. She also announced a due date in February 2015. Because I was tracking dates and possibilities so closely, I looked at that and said, "She must be like... one day pregnant!" I went to bed that night and dreamed of her. Nothing specific, just my friend and babies and a blur that held when I woke up, and when a dream stays with me, I tend to know it has meaning. And so that day, I just knew I was pregnant too.

Rod said I should wait to take a test. It was really early, and though he didn't say it, he was really worried. We'd told ourselves we'd give it all of 2014 to get pregnant again, come what may, but I had already confessed how unsettling it was to think we wouldn't have another baby. I did not want my childbearing chapter to end with a miscarriage.

Swerve

I am normally pretty submissive to my husband, but that Tuesday, on the way to work, I stopped and bought a pregnancy test. My heart was racing. I needed to know (I'm an information addict). There was a five-minute drive to the church office where I worked. I played one song: Crystal Lewis, "Lord I Believe in You." Crystal's range is far higher than mine. I sang along anyway. I might have shouted.

Because once again, I found myself in a place where I needed to choose to believe.

Even if this story didn't play out how I wanted, Jesus loves me.

Even if I don't see a joyful ending or a hopeful next chapter, even if my childbearing years end with loss instead of life, God already performed amazing miracles – giving an infertile woman *three* babies, two on earth and one in Heaven. It would be okay.

And it was okay. I walked into work, stepped into the public bathroom in the empty lower level, took the test. I wish I could say I was surprised when it was POSITIVE, but somewhere in the midst of the nine preceding years, from infertility diagnosis to two babies to miscarriage, I'd become a hopeFUL person instead of a cynical one. God had already confirmed in that dream about my sweet pregnant friend that I was pregnant too. I hung up and called Rod (who also wasn't surprised I'd taken the test and who laughed with me on the phone), I called my mom. (*She is so used to me. Thank you for knowing me,*

Mama). And then I marched upstairs and told all my co-workers, who had loved me so well through my miscarriage and were a safe place.

I was something like… three weeks?… pregnant at that point. Common sense and a million pregnancy articles would have told me to wait to tell anyone. Crystal Lewis and amazing grace told me to SHOUT THAT OUT. God was giving me life after loss.

Life, abundantly.

I will tell you that the following weeks were a battle of my mind. There were some days of spotting, and even one night of some bleeding. There were moments I could not stop my imagination from running wild. There were days of not only fear but of guilt and grief – I still very much missed and mourned our David (*I still do!*).

I had some amazing people pray with me, including an impromptu *call down the fire* at a Pampered Chef party that I will never forget that (*Thank you forever, Chris!*). I had a sweet surrogate dad send me Bible verses and songs right when I needed them most (*Junie. I love you!*) I received a prophecy of a pea-pod, sprouting forth with life (*Kelli! Words of life!*). I had a playlist of songs to affirm me, which I listened to over and over again. I had a husband, my champion, tell me over and over again that no matter what, I was going to be okay.

On June 26, I had an ultrasound scheduled. For the 24 hours before, my heart raced and my stomach churned. I was relieved that my girls were in Illinois with my parents. I flashed myself forward to scenarios of celebration as well as grief. I prayed and declared victory and life. I thanked God for the person inside me, even as I held that little person at a distance.

My first ultrasound with David had been a nightmare. At first,

Dr. M. couldn't find an embryo at all (turns out my uterus was tilted). Then there was a baby who was smaller than he should have been and whose heartbeat wasn't visible. I was confused, embarrassed, angry, and quite quickly broken.

※

This time... oh wow. I have told people about the song in my head in those seconds leading to the ultrasound:

"*We wait for you.*
We wait for you.
We wait for you to fill the room."
(Thomas, Hacket, Asbury, et al).

The song talks about Holy Spirit. I was, of course, waiting to see my baby, but it was both of them who greeted me the moment I looked at the screen. Now an ultrasound veteran, I immediately saw a heartbeat flashing beautifully. I immediately felt the reassuring presence of a life-giving God fill the room. I cried and said, "Thank You, Jesus" over and over again.

I was something like nine weeks along at that point. There was still a long way to go in my pregnancy, and there would still be battles of fear and worry to face, but I declared life.

And I would do it all over again.

Can we declare baby news too soon? Does shouting good news somehow jinx it? To this I say: *Sometimes you have to battle fear by calling it out.* For me, I had to declare life quickly and loudly and to everyone.

Our faith does not change situations all by itself. I could have just as easily lost another baby (*a story to be continued*). In fact, that friend, the one who I dreamed about, lost one of her precious twins, born six days before my Jack, at nine weeks old. Loss and life are intermingled in ways we cannot even fathom. But God made us to persevere, to live, and to love even through the darkest tragedies. When I see my friend smiling at her children, functioning through her grief, I am in awe of her spirit and of the God who sustains her.

There will always be loss. But there will always, always be life on the other side.

Swerve: Loss is devastating. There is no sugarcoating it. There is also no hiding from it.

Consider: How can we keep moving forward after grief has struck our lives? What help does God offer to us?

Live: In the hardest times, the simple act of believing in the goodness and faithfulness of God, even when our senses and emotions tell us everything is bad, is enough. Simply believe, and allow Him to do the rest of the work.

17. Blending Families

happily-ever-afters for complicated relationships

"GOD IS BUILDING A HOME. HE'S USING US ALL—IRRESPEC-
TIVE OF HOW WE GOT HERE—IN WHAT HE IS BUILDING."
FROM EPHESIANS 2:19-22 MSG

I meant to text you this past Sunday. I wore shorts to church.

My now-grown bonus son smirked at me. No other words were needed. Not so many years ago, whether it was holy and acceptable to wear shorts to church had been one of many lines in the sand drawn between us. Both of us growing up, moving to the beach, learning about grace, had changed everything between us.

Josh is but one complicated relationship in my life that has led to a happily-ever-after. When I married his dad, I was 26 and he was 11. I thought because I'd grown up with a brother, I would know all about the mind of an adolescent boy. I thought because I was a cool auntie, that I would be a wise and beloved mother figure. I thought I knew what it meant to inherit a family when I married my husband. I was wrong on all these fronts.

The beginning of our marriage was fraught with unmet

expectations. Turns out, loving kids and theorizing about how to raise them is pretty darn different than living in the muck of adolescent hormones, young hearts broken and confused by divorce, and years of dysfunctional communication and co-dependent relationships (*theirs, mine, ours!*). The beginning years of my marriage to Rod were fraught with missteps, tension, and arguments, 90 percent of which stemmed from our different ideas – and unrealistic expectations – about bringing up kids and blending a family together.

Living in the beautiful mess of that was so intense and exhausting, even though, in the thick of it, I knew we weren't doing so bad. Trust me, when you've had a crazy romantic history (homeless guys, addicted guys, imprisoned guys...), and you marry a man with an adulterous past, a first wife living three blocks away, young kids, and plenty of bitter ex-friends, you hear every second marriage/blended family horror story there is. Some anonymous kind hearts even clip them out of magazines and mail them to you! Though now I know comparison is counter-productive, there were days that ended with me thinking, "At least it's not as bad as...." At least we weren't quite fit for a Danielle Steele novel or an episode of *Dallas*. At least a few of the school teachers and friend's parents would deal with The Stepmom.

And you know, at least those kids and I loved each other.

There is a lot of water under the bridge of those early years. There are conversations, blow-ups, and events that were so utterly momentous at the time that *I have forgotten about* until Rod, Josh, or Paige remind me. It's kind of like writing a book, when you are putting those first pages out with the concentrated force of a drowning person gasping for air, trying to get everything out, everything right, everything oxygenated and healthy and alive before you lose it. Rod and I dove head first into creating a family together because it was *all we wanted*. Sometimes we overlooked important details or made decisions for the wrong reasons or the wrong outcome.

But never, ever did we doubt the worth of our cause:
A happily ever after.

We have been married over 16 years as I write this (19 as I prepare to publish!). That little boy who just wanted to wear shorts to church is now a top car salesman who wears dress pants *and* dress shoes to work every day. He has a child of his own, a wife, a house, a life with its own complications, tensions, joys, victories. His little sister has grown into a lovely, capable woman who is forging and re-forging her own path and is one of my very best friends. I could not be prouder of them or more grateful that we believed in a fairy tale *when everything told us we were crazy*.

But I have to add a post-script to the happily ever after, because there were months my stepson did not talk to me. There were decisions his sister made that made me think, *Did we cause this?* There were years their mom and I did not speak to each other at all. There are people who never could forgive Rod and me for daring to make this family; some even went to their graves never seeing the redemption God gave to us.

But we four stayed together, and we have grown. The kids' mom is now someone I consider a sister… someone my three biological children call "auntie." She always has a seat at our table. I never imagined we would *all* be a family; I barely dared to hope it. Now, we are makeshift poster children for blended families.

The key to all of this, *all of it*, friends, is forgiveness and grace. Blended families, God help us, are not the perfect design. They are not anyone's goal when they first fall in love and make commitments. But they happen. They happen like mashed potatoes with way too many of way too hard lumps. Or they happen like Steak n' Shake's finest blend of milk, ice cream, and dark chocolate syrup. It all depends on the decision to forgive each other and ourselves and to extend grace to every single person in that family. (Yes, even the kids need it sometimes, because they can become masters of manipulation and guilt-tripping when armed properly!)

Without that grace, any family, really, is left with baggage, bitterness, regret, hostility, and holiday seasons that bring eggshell-walking, lumps of anxiety like proverbial coal, and something like a Vince Vaughn/Reese Witherspoon catastrophic hodge-podge. Who wants that?

So much of my life began with the choice to pursue the complicated relationship of being a second wife and stepmom. So much of my wisdom has come from the hard lessons it took to figure that out. So much of the joy in my life comes from the foundational family that my husband and my two *bonus* kids made together.

God's Word is simple: He is for wholeness, for holiness, for love. Our lives are complicated, so when we need to *swerve* – a sudden shift from a dangerous road, a rerouting after a catastrophic collision, He allows us to apply some of the other gifts He's stored up for us: peace, patience, kindness, gentleness, self-control. And grace.

There is always grace.

And it makes for the best kind of happily-ever-afters.

Swerve: God makes strangers into family – we are all His family!

Consider: What complicated relationship exists in your life? What are your beliefs about why it is that way and whether it can change?

Live: Reach beyond your insecurities, doubts, and hurt feelings, and extend grace to the person on the other end of that complicated relationship. In your search for understanding and peace, may you find a happily ever after.

18. Realistic Romance

both sides of Johnny Castle

"MY LITTLE CHILDREN, LET US NOT LOVE IN WORD, NEITHER IN TONGUE; BUT IN DEED AND IN TRUTH." 1 JOHN 3:18 KJV

Usually I believe it to be a beautiful thing: the way time colors and shifts our perspective into something refined, something that makes sense out of the past, something that finds the reason for it all or the lesson learned.

But one night, after watching the 1987 hit movie *Dirty Dancing* for perhaps the 17-millionth time, I felt the opposite. Because after watching that time, I feel a little blame-y toward Johnny Castle.

Oh, don't get me wrong. As played by Patrick Swayze, sweet, sexy, swoon-worthy graceful-yet-macho, left-us-way-too-soon Hollywood icon for my generation and others, he remains one of the most romantic leading men of the 1980s, and probably ever.

But as an archetype for a mate, a boyfriend, a first love, the thirty-something mommy version of me said, No way.

It's no wonder we fell for him, my Gen X sisters. Not only

was he smoldering in every version of tight black shirt he donned in the film, he was sensitive. He had a passion to dance, rather than join the housepainter's union. He was a supportive, responsible hero to his 'friend' Penny. (Though, give me a break... even the junior high version of me knew Penny would have been more than friends with Johnny faster than you can say "Kellerman's"). And Johnny looked at Baby the way a suburban mom with three kids in the car looks at a Panera Bread with a drive-thru, as if she personified hope, kindness, solace, and a one-way ticket out of sure misery.

But, dude. She was 17. (There is some conjecture about whether she was actually 18. I am sticking to my guns, here, because even if... this all still applies!) Seventeen. And though the magazine told us it's where the girl ends and the woman begins, and the Winger song says she'll show you love like you've never seen, 17 was one year younger than my oldest daughter then, (slightly older than my youngest now), the age I was when I made some of the worst decisions of my life, and only half the age I was then, and at 34, still feeling like I knew next-to-nothing most days.

Seventeen is not fit to be anyone's romantic hero, at least not in middle class America.

Seventeen is look-don't-touch to a twentysomething guy, no matter how *noble* he is.

And quite frankly, considering a week before he met Baby, he was accepting the room keys of several random older women a day, I'm not sure noble is a good term for him.

(I still adore you, Johnny Castle, and I still mourn you, Patrick Swayze, but...)

You are not a guy I want my daughters to love. (Though you're a guy I'd want my husband to mentor.)

And watching you at junior high slumber parties, repeatedly

rewinding the part when you scrunch your adorable nose and sing, "And I owe it all to you" is probably one of the reasons I had my own ridiculous, soap-operaesque 'save the males' romantic complex during my dating years.

(Though I still love listening to "She's Like the Wind" on repeat sometimes...)

And really, would it have been that hard for you to say to Dr. Houseman from the onset that you were taking responsibility for Penny, not that you were responsible for her pregnancy and botched, horrible, illegal abortion? Would that not have been easier than expecting a 17-year-old Daddy's girl to stand up for you?

(Though, seriously, then we wouldn't have had a movie or a "Nobody Puts Baby In The Corner" onesie for our own babies...)

At the end of this particular viewing of *Dirty Dancing*, my mom, sister-in-law, Facebook friends and I debated whether Johnny and Baby ended up together after the movie. Through 20 years of watching, I'd always just kind of assumed they did.

How can you have the ultimate love story if the lovers aren't together forever?

How can you have the time of your life and then just walk away from it? But on the flip side, how can a sheltered 17-year-old heading off to college and the peace corps so dramatically change the course of her life in the 1960s that she ends up marrying a sometimes-employed, older dancer from New York? Does he become a housepainter to impress her dad with his stability? Does she give up her status and family to travel the

Merengue circuit as his partner? Do they buy a VW minibus, declare themselves hippies, shuck the establishment, and grow up to be Steven and Elyse Keaton a la *Family Ties*?

I can't imagine any of those scenarios.

As I watched the movie, it was all too easy to remember the passion and temptation of infatuation, the delicious anticipation of new love - and the mysterious, misleading adventure of forbidden love. Does it work out sometimes?

Well, honestly, in real life, I married a version of Johnny Castle - and he looks really good in a black shirt, and he is the best husband I could have, and he's an amazing provider and daddy to our kids, but the Johnny Castle model of romance is not the one I'd order up for my daughters. Because even though it is a beautiful notion that love rescues, that love redeems, that love conquers all, love in the real world carries baggage and consequences and most of the time, the world is not very forgiving to the Johnnys and Babys.

Love all you can, but keep the restraints on until you know,

until you aren't 17, and until there is nothing about it you are compelled to hide.

God didn't just create love; He is love, and because He is also light, love that exists in darkness cannot lead to a happy ending.

Swerve: Nothing makes you grow out of youthful romantic fantasies like having your children exposed to or indulging in the same ones!

Consider: Some of us know real life Johnnys and Babys; maybe are even raising them. So guide your children, and have grace for others.

Live: It's ideal to model Godly romantic love to our kids. If this is not feasible in your situation, intentionally find ways to show your children what it looks like.

19. Reckless Love

the ultimate romantic hero

"REMAIN IN ME, AND I WILL REMAIN IN YOU. FOR A BRANCH CANNOT PRODUCE FRUIT IF IT IS SEVERED FROM THE VINE, AND YOU CANNOT BE FRUITFUL UNLESS YOU REMAIN IN ME."
JOHN 15:4 NLT

"YOUR GREATEST STRENGTH USED IN EXCESS BECOMES YOUR GREATEST WEAKNESS." UNKNOWN

The idea of strength becoming weakness has always been a confirmation and a warning to me. Because the easiest thing in the world for me is to fall in love with people and love them big. But for much of my life, I've loved the wrong way – with the desire to be seen, special, appreciated, and of course, loved in return. And if I'm being honest, in many cases, I wanted to be loved "the most."

I have often analyzed the cause of this phenomenon, even though each of us has one, don't we? Culture will call it a personality type of some sort (I didn't have to study deeply to label myself an Enneagram 2). One fascinating theory is second-born syndrome, the sects of which I often identified, even more so when I became a second wife. A study on spiritual gifts was also like a mirror: clearly, my prominent gift is compassion, and as my Pastor once summarized it, "Compassion People have no sense." That would be funny if it wasn't, when compassion is not coupled with wisdom, completely true.

The results of this desire are fairly textbook. I spent time in high school trying to impress the wrong "friends" and "rescue" the wrong guys. When I finally started to grasp the damage that M.O. was causing, I switched to another misguided love mission – trying to convince "good people" (mainly church folks and relatives) that I had become Acceptable.

I never truly succeeded in those attempts.

Because God is good and life tends to be a little balanced...

...there were real friendships that were positive and lasting. There were Good People who never gave up on me, too. And despite every odd against me, him, and us, there was a romantic hero with whom I've lived and am living that modern fairy tale: We rescued each other.

Growing up and making a family of my own and being fairly stabilized took a lot of those tendencies away from me. I've done a lot less chasing, save for when –

- I wanted to be accepted as a parent, by my stepkids and by the community around us
- I wanted to find my place in the workforce after stepping backing to be a full-time mama and then also, an entrepreneur.
- I desperately sought new *real friends* and a makeshift family in a brand-new town.

- Anyone who was previously a close relationship began to drift for any reason whatsoever...

Each of these circumstances flared up that muscle memory, that chink in my armor, that wanted to prove I was worthy, love until I was loved back. I had to learn to uncomfortably stretch those compassionate muscles past their memories and reach for the source of the compassion I felt, to Jesus, who not only gave it to me, but set the example for how to apply it. Compassion without wisdom, without connection to the ultimate Giver of Love, is easily turned into a weakness or even a weapon.

As I made my way into my 40s, I became more aware of this, more willing to believe it. You see, the part of me that wants to be loved the most had to come to terms with the truth offered in scripture and expressed beautifully in a popular worship song: Jesus *does* love me the most:

> *"There's no shadow You won't light up, mountain You won't climb up, coming after me. There's no wall You won't kick down, life You won't tear down, coming after me. Oh, the overwhelming, never-ending, reckless love of God. Oh, it chases me down, fights 'til I'm found, leaves the ninety-nine..."*
> *- Caleb Culver / Cory Hunter Asbury / Randy Matthew Jackson, "Reckless Love."*

I think the battle of *using* versus *losing* to our greatest strength is wholly lifelong. I'm grateful to be learning the voice of God, alerting me when I'm about to step where I shouldn't or ask a person for something only He can provide and already did! And I am grateful for a husband and a few stalwart friends who aren't afraid to poke, prod, tease, or shake me when I'm going sideways, giving too much of myself away in misguided quests for Big Love.

These days, when I hear "Reckless Love," I can't help but smile. I think of Michael Douglas' character Jack Colton in *Romancing the Stone*, cutting overgrown branches with his machete to clear a path for Kathleen Turner's Joan Wilder, swinging her across turbulent waters on a vine, or wrestling a crocodile to recover a treasure they thought they'd lost. Maybe my husband would do all those things for me; I know he would be willing to try. But no one has to do the chasing, the kicking, the fighting, the questing. Not you or me or the romantic interests before us. Jesus already did. He is the ultimate romantic hero.

Swerve: God made you and your strengths. Let Him guide you in how you apply them.

Consider: Because God loves you so much, He will protect your heart, even when it leads you astray. Don't be afraid to depend on Him to be faithful in the everyday and to rescue you when you need it.

Live: Because God protects our hearts, we *can* love others lavishly, without expectation, and know that He will always love us even more in return.

20. Miscarriage Part 3

God said LIVE

"THE SPIRIT OF GOD, WHO RAISED JESUS FROM THE DEAD, LIVES IN YOU. AND JUST AS GOD RAISED CHRIST JESUS FROM THE DEAD, HE WILL GIVE LIFE TO YOUR MORTAL BODIES BY THIS SAME SPIRIT LIVING WITHIN YOU."
ROMANS 8:11 NLT

"EVEN IF I DON'T SEE A JOYFUL ENDING OR A HOPEFUL NEXT CHAPTER, EVEN IF MY CHILDBEARING YEARS END WITH LOSS INSTEAD OF LIFE, GOD ALREADY PERFORMED AMAZING MIRACLES – GIVING AN INFERTILE WOMAN THREE BABIES, TWO ON EARTH AND ONE IN HEAVEN. IT WOULD BE OKAY."
- THIS BOOK, 'MISCARRIAGE PART 2'

So I had Jack in January of 2015, and he is the exclamation point, the rainbow baby, the joy-bringer, the redemption child. Everything about his birth was a redeeming experience, and everything about his personality has lived up to the celebration of his arrival.

As women who have experienced only C-section births can attest, it feels like a bit of a robbery not to have your baby without this major medical intervention. During my pregnancy with Jack, I was in a program called Centering, which involved group appointments with a midwife and workshops that boosted my confidence to breastfeed, to try cloth diapers, to chill the heck out and just love my baby well. I was in this program with a fellow mama of a rainbow baby, who happened to be my daughter's dance teacher, and though I was the oldest mama in there, I felt so inspired by who surrounded me. Even my midwife had a complicated reproduction story. She made me feel so empowered.

I thought maybe I could talk someone, anyone, into letting me try for a vaginal birth. It was not to be. So I had the next best thing: a "gentle" C-section, which meant if all was well, I could hold my baby immediately, and as a bonus, my midwife said she would be there with me. This meant even more in those few difficult minutes of pre-op when the spinal block process was not going so well. Maureen held my hand through it all. When Jack was born and he was finally in my arms and looking for his milk (I still marvel at this miraculous design), she and Rod were off to the side chatting, just on the peripheral of my magical bubble with my baby boy.

Also during these moments, Dr. M. was performing a tubal ligation; in a nutshell, my fallopian tubes were cut and burned (I could smell it. I was so happy, it didn't even faze me) to prevent future pregnancies. At this point, Rod was nearing 51, I was nearing 40, and while we had welcomed a chance to *start over, again*, we were finished. Complete. D-O-N-E.

December. I was living the crazed mom life. We'd decided to homeschool the girls for a while. I was still working part time at our church. Jack was nursing like a pro and had taken to the attachment parenting *very* well, the only of our children who co-slept with us. Rod traveled a lot for work. I said yes to everything. In December, we involved ourselves in not one or two but *three* Christmas productions and a fairly big baking project for a Christmas party at the family shelter.

During this time, Jack also decided to nurse like a newborn. I loved breastfeeding; it was another key piece in the redemption story of his birth and babydom. But he regressed during the holiday season. He needed more of me. It was perplexing, but we moved on through it. And right after the holidays, we left for a big, extended family trip to Disney World.

During our last morning at the park, Rod and I decided we should go ahead and get annual passes. The kids had so much fun. We'd done it before and enjoyed it. We just had to stop at a particular building in the Magic Kingdom and renew them in person, or something. That detail is fuzzy. What isn't fuzzy is the strange Jedi-like mind thing that happened after we made that decision. Suddenly, we were in our minivan, going home. Without another word to each other, we never stopped to get the tickets renewed. And I was doing math in my head and realized that in December, my monthly cycle never came. And I knew, just like I had known with Jack, that I was pregnant.

Sometimes, even if not often, Holy Spirit works that way. For some reason, it works that way with me and pregnancies. The knowledge of those little lives inside me dropped like truth in my soul before a test ever told me "YES." This time was different. This time, there was really *no way*. And yet. I cannot remember how long we waited, but I think it was just a few days. And then: BAM. We got that "Yes." But it was different.

I wasn't sure I wanted to be pregnant again.

Life was crazy. How could we add another whole person to it?

We'd already done the "two under two" thing, and I was *older*. Rod was *older*. Could we really do it again?

Medically speaking, there was a bit of a rush to get me in for an ultrasound. The chances of an ectopic – potentially fatal – pregnancy are high after a tubal ligation. I was sent to the hospital for an ultrasound, during which the tech would not let us see the screen and told us absolutely nothing. We would know nothing for 24 hours.

Midwife Maureen texted me on and off during this time. She was as reassuring as one could be. But even her voice was not enough to bring me peace. I knew what I needed.

That afternoon, in the time of waiting, I held a sleeping Jack in the rocking chair of his bedroom, a room and a chair we rarely used, because he was always with us, in our room, in our arms. As I slept, I talked to Jesus. I told him I was sorry for my doubts, because *of course* we wanted this child. I looked around the room and pictured how we could move things to accommodate a baby brother or sister. And out loud, I told that little baby that we welcomed him. That he was wanted.

The ultrasound showed a viable baby, in the right place. So we made plans. We upgraded ourselves to a king-sized bed, just in case we ended up with two co-sleepers. We moved a twin bed to Jack's room and left the crib (I have some great pictures of this day). We made a funny meme with the *Brady Bunch* title, because what could be funnier than us having six kids?

We had two follow-up appointments. Both of them showed a strong, beating heart. Dr. M. was flabbergasted. Maureen was happy to be along for the ride, even as she was preparing for her own possible pregnancy. We choose the name Jesse for a boy, or Jessie for a girl. It means "gift" and "God exists." We accepted our future. We had room.

And then, just like two years before, right around our Kaity's birthday, I started spotting.

And just like that Jedi Holy Spirit moment when I knew I was pregnant, I knew Jesse was gone.

Swerve

Oh, I went through the motions. I made Kaity's birthday happy. I took the tags off a $70 maternity dress and wore it, as an act of faith. I laid my hands on my stomach and earnestly declared resurrection. I texted with Maureen and let her reassure me. I prayed and cried and prayed and prayed and prayed.

And we went to the appointment that Monday, and Maureen could not find a heartbeat. And she said – I will never forget it – "With your uterus, this baby could be anywhere!" Oh, LOL. We walked downstairs to where the ultrasound machine was. A doctor who was not Dr. M. and whose name I happily forget very clinically hooked me up, questioned whether I was ever actually pregnant at all, and read my chart, seeing that I'd had a tubal ligation 13 months prior. She looked at Maureen and said,

> "These are very unusual circumstances for a pregnancy."

Oh, how Rod and I laughed. We laughed until we cried, while that doctor stared in bewilderment at Maureen. What was *wrong* with these people, anyway?

The rest of the story starts with sadness. There was no heartbeat. Though I'd carried Jesse for 11 weeks, he'd stopped growing around seven weeks, probably dying a day or so after we last saw his heartbeat. I still required a D&C; my babies do not like to leave my body without surgical assistance, apparently. During that procedure, Dr. M. also performed a salpingectomy, which removed my fallopian tubes entirely.

The procedure was physically harder than I expected. And the aftermath was harder, too. My grief was made much more difficult because I tried to hide it. I didn't want my daughters to know, so I held them at a distance (I had to work really hard to forgive myself for this). I didn't tell my friends. I let Rod know, and I nursed Jack like a champ. That is what anchored me, which was not enough to sustain me. Occasionally, I cried out to my pastors or even yelled at them (a perk of being on church staff, perhaps...) because WHAT GOOD WAS FAITH IF IT IS TO NO EFFECT?

I *prayed* with faith bigger than a mustard seed.

I *believed* that the same resurrection power that raised Jesus from the dead dwells in me.

And I wasn't mad at God, but clearly, He was going to do what He wanted anyway, so *what was the point*?

For nearly an entire year, I stopped praying. I didn't stop believing in God. I just embraced my own powerlessness, and I no longer saw the point in asking Him for anything or even agreeing with His word. The cards were gonna fall however they were going to, and I just needed the grace to accept it.

That's what I told myself. I had a lot to learn. I asked hard questions during that hard year. I mean, 2016 was filled with awful crap, and this had happened in February. Hiding grief and carrying anger through it all was not helpful to anyone, least of all me. But God never left my side. He's big enough for our tough questions. He can handle our doubts, even when they last for months. He does not retaliate when we give Him the silent treatment. He cries with us. And guess what else? He *trusts* us to get through it on the other side, stronger. That's what a good Father does.

We will not always be rescued from the hard things. My faith questions *still* are not all answered. Every time someone loses a baby in utero or out, I wince and find myself whisper-screaming *WHY?!* I have learned that reaping and sowing are not a tit-for-tat trade. The world is fallen. Bad things happen that cannot be attributed to any one thing. And... if I believe God formed us in the womb, then I also have to accept that Jesse had a soul, a chooser, a choice. I accept that my baby was presented with the choice to stay in this unpredictable, often painful world (with his mama and his awesome family) or bypass it and wait for us in paradise with his Maker and his brother David. To some, that will sound like a fantasy. To me, it is a comforting truth.

Because even if I didn't get the joyful ending, even if my childbearing years ended with loss instead of life, God already performed amazing miracles – giving an infertile woman five babies, three on earth and two in Heaven.

And it is okay*.

Swerve: When life throws curves, God still says LIVE. And He still wants us to live life abundantly.

Consider: God has given the world free choice. This means there are consequences, losses, tragedies, heartbreaks that are not controlled by us and still not attributed to Him. He is our Savior; He waits for us to choose Him.

Live: This part of my story did not end how I wanted, how I prayed. But it's one chapter, not the whole thing. I will forever use God's redemption to encourage others; He will get us through the things we never thought we could withstand.

*Redeem: While I was pregnant with Jesse, my sister-friend Shannon and I made up stories of how fun it would be to have two little boys in the family, only 21 months apart. Shannon, like I once did, thought she would never have children. She is also a stepmom, and she and her husband have been foster parents for years *(as told in chapter 14, "Helplessnsess")*. While in the long arduous process of adopting baby boy Carlito and his three older sisters, they were quite miraculously and easily rewarded custody of another baby boy, Max.

Carlito and Max are 21 months apart. Our family will see that vision come to life. ***God redeems ALL things in His time, in His way.***

21. The Year 2020

God Said *Swerve*

"THE THIEF COMETH NOT, BUT FOR TO STEAL, AND TO KILL, AND TO DESTROY: I AM COME THAT THEY MIGHT HAVE LIFE, AND THAT THEY MIGHT HAVE IT MORE ABUNDANTLY."
JOHN 10:10 KJV

When I first began putting together this book, showing how grace helped me make quick turns in life's unexpected curves, I thought I had a pretty good handle on the meaning of "swerve."

And then, before I could hit the proverbial "Publish" button, March 2020 came around.

Where were you when it started? I was on a cruise ship with my husband. At the time I write this, it ended up being the last cruise leaving out of Port Charleston, South Carolina for who knows how long. Oh, we had the time of our lives. The ship was half-empty, the crew was cleaning like crazy, and blissfully, we were not watching any news at all.

Then word started trickling in from home. Red alerts were issued. Schools were closed. *Disney World* was even considering a shutdown. I heard from my job, a local running store, that we would mitigate procedures as the week went along, canceling our group runs and ramping up cleaning protocols. There was a *small* flicker of worry in my head that our ship might be quarantined when we reached the shore (it was not). Other than that, we shrugged... survivors of the swine flu scare and several hurricane evacuations... and figured if anything, the kids would be home driving us crazy for a few weeks.

We all know how that played out, don't we? But I will not be taking this story "there." No. I want to look at some of the *essential* heroes that didn't quite get celebrated with social media frames and filters and commercials and t-shirts: the small business heroes who managed to swerve like, well, nobody's business.

It was, in fact, the time of pandemic that made me fully realize how much I always have believed in *small business*. Growing up in a small suburban area, every teen got her first job at one of them. I can count mine off and remember the names of so many bosses and co-workers and even customers, at Marvell Bakery, Dari Whip, Flower Depot, Scott's U-Save Tires. Each of those businesses taught me a whole lot about the commitment it takes to run one, the personality and energy it takes to attract and keep customers, the fine art of surrounding oneself with people who invest in your vision, the gut checks necessary to rebound from hardships.

Working in a church for nearly 10 years showed me more of the same. Though churches are set up to be families, they have to run as local businesses as well, with communication and logistics often being the practical backbone as much as Jesus and love are the spiritual one. Our church happened to be meeting in a school when the pandemic shut down all government buildings. We were effectively homeless and, at that time, we were not yet livestreaming our services.

What do small businesses do when they cannot invite customers into their buildings?

What do churches do when they have no locale and need the internet bells and whistles to reach their people?

Why, yes.

They swerve.

In a whirlwind time, a time when many people were living an extreme of being stuck inside their homes to accomplish any and every thing, or working endlessly in something like health care or education or grocery stores, the local businesses were smack-dab in the middle: trying to figure out new means to serve *and* to survive... quickly!

Suddenly, our traditional brick-and-mortar running store, with a specialty of fitting customers in shoes to optimize their time on their feet, was scanning hundreds of items into inventory for online sales and exhaustively conversing with clients over the phone to fit them for curbside or at times, home delivery of their new shoes.

Our church was offered space in a local restaurant (because, you know, no one was allowed to eat there) to video our services. We had to figure out how to livestream with the equipment we had and upgrade it so that it didn't look horrible. We also had to find a way to best communicate the balance of taking a new virus strain seriously and keeping faith in a time of fear.

It was a heavy time. I was surrounded, in both of my jobs, by the unknown. I was working closely with people who were usually steady but are also human and had to fight daily against the fear of that unknown, how to proceed with operations, how they would be perceived, how their livelihood would survive.

I watched the two businesses I am a part of make it. I got to be a part of that, and it's my "2020 Legacy." I was there for people who had to swerve. I helped swerve. Swerving took innovation, trial and error, and bravery. It took coming together and asking for help when needed. It took patience with people who didn't see things the same way but wanted the same outcome.

It also took a new mantra for me, heard in a song*, to decide what my role would be in my jobs, my community, and my family. In one of the four different locales we used for church before we settled into a closed Books-a-Million for our *home for now* space, I first heard the Elevation Worship song called "Rattle" on a Sunday morning.

It spoke to every part of me: the fear, the hope, the anxiety, the drive. I didn't want to be afraid, and I was angry because society was telling me every hour of every day to let fear rule me. So "God said live" became my reason for living within my family and community in a way we agreed was honorable, safe, uplifting, healthy, necessary, and abundant. Yes, indeed --

God said live.

I struggled many days with how to live and swerve during that time. While my family remained healthy and employed and in personal fellowship with a circle of people, so many around us struggled. We had *two* friends with bedridden spouses who had trouble getting the supplies or medical care they needed. We had friends who couldn't get home or whose adult children couldn't get home. Friends who worked in the music industry suddenly had no job to do. Friends who lost loved ones and could have no real funeral (one of the most humbling tasks I had during all of 2020 was "producing" several online funerals). And who of us didn't suffer from and/or watch our kids and/or parents suffer from some form of depression?

My answer to swerving was to keep doing what I was doing,

but more of it. When someone was discouraged, I learned to encourage them without hesitation. When someone needed a meal, we brought one, ordered one, or found someone else to share one. When someone asked for a hug, I gave it, and when they asked for an air hug, I faked it!

And I learned. I learned how to compartmentalize my big emotions, because they were not only big, but scattered all over the place. And this led to one very important lesson for me:

I learned to sit in sacred silence.

I learned that some things just can't be solved with my typical specialty, the pep talk. So I sat in that silence alongside the sorrowful depths of a grieving mother, a friend in chronic pain, the ones mentioned above, and sometimes, my own family in their disappointments and loneliness.

Swerving looked like so many things in 2020. It did not always look pretty or even victorious, but it was necessary to gutting through a year that will be one of the hardest for many of us who lived through it. And just like always, the journey was so much about how we navigated to our destination rather than the destination itself. In fact, it will be months or years before we truly know how the twists and turns of the 2020 swerve have impacted our lives and our world. For now, we keep going one step at a time, following the turns, helping others along, always moving forward.

Swerve: Life "abundantly" doesn't only mean good abundance, but sometimes an abundance of complications, turmoil, and challenges.

Consider: We don't always have to find a silver lining in a dark cloud, but in faith, we can find the lesson learned or the strength for tomorrow.

Live: Jesus said Himself that He came to give us LIFE. His Spirit equips us to live through all the seasons of it.

Resources:

For a deeper understanding of the love of Jesus, the gospel, grace, the New Covenant, and living in God's life, abundantly, I highly recommend these resources:

Clash Of The Covenants: Escaping Religious Bondage Through The Grace Guarantee
by Michael C. Kapler

*The Rest of the Gospel:
When the Partial Gospel Has Worn You Out*
by Dan Stone and David Gregory

*Why I Rejected Religion:
A Walk Through Romans*
by Thomas W. Wallace II with Bev Swanson
(coming in 2022)

For miscarriage support:

stillbirthday.com

Special Thanks

My husband and anchor, Rod Burton

My Mom & Dad

My sister-friend Deanna Mason

The staff of Journeychurch, my covenant co-workers for 10 years

My advance readers: Vicki Hicks, Michael Hopkins, Dana Anderson, Mylena Yee, Sarah Barrentine, Kenny Bishop, & always, Shannon Montano

All the friends in various faith walks who are willing to have the tough conversations. I trust you know who you are, and I am so grateful we can listen and love through the hard work of trying to understand.

My children, grandchild, and nieces and nephews

All the lighthouses

About the Author

Kelly Capriotti Burton is a wife, mama, bonus mom, daughter, gigi, sister-friend, auntie, & pastor. While she holds those roles most dear, she has found "life, abundantly" working as a running store manager and author. She resides with her family in Surfside Beach, South Carolina.

Also by Kelly

THE SURFSIDE BEACH SERIES:
The Tentative Knock
Another at the Table

Coming November 2022: Run This Way

Thank you!

Readers:
Your reviews mean more than you know. If you liked what you read, consider leaving a rating or review at the retailer of your choice, Amazon, and/or Goodreads.

I'd love to stay in touch!
Please subscribe at kellofastory.com
& give a follow on Facebook or Instagram at
@kellofastory

Made in the USA
Columbia, SC
27 September 2024